ENGLISH PENNY

Penelope Fyvel

ARTHUR H. STOCKWELL LTD.
Elms Court   Ilfracombe   Devon
Established 1898

To My Husband Mick

ISBN 0 7223 2648-3

Printed in Great Britain by
Arthur H. Stockwell Ltd.
Elms Court   Ilfracombe
Devon

CONTENTS

Part V

'And to Make an End is to Make a Beginning'

LIST OF ILLUSTRATIONS

FOREWORD

Through Rough Ways to the Stars

Motto of Hillcroft College

"English Penny" was born in 1939 when I recounted to the late T. R. Fyvel, a writer and my brother-in-law, experiences of a Tottenham childhood and as a nurse in the Spanish Civil War. Outbreak of World War II, however, caused the manuscript to be laid aside.

Fifty years on I have resumed my story. Chapters on my childhood and Spain have been curtailed. The lives of working-class families in the earlier parts of the century have been well documented, while radio and television have added to the printed word. Likewise, many books on the Spanish Civil War have appeared. What happened to me after leaving school with practically no education may be relevant today when apparently so many young people are in a similar situation. Prince Charles recently stressed the importance of young people receiving advice as to their future. I was fortunate in obtaining such advice, which steered me towards nursing. *"English Penny"* is not meant to be an autobiography, but a chronicle of the way in which war, medicine and social change shaped my life.

On returning home in 1938 after being wounded in Spain, I received many letters from well-wishers. These I could not acknowledge then, but I would like to do so now, better late perhaps, than never. I hope I have not dwelt too much on my medical problems subsequent to bomb-blast injury. It takes a long time, however, sometimes a very long time, to get over such serious injury.

6

Through *"English Penny"* I wish to pay tribute to nurses and social workers. The Spanish people on the Republican side were the first to face dictators while we were still wobbling; their sacrifice at that time deserves recall. Now Spain is a flourishing democratic state. Nearly a million Britons have made their home there, creating a strong link between our two countries. The British, too, should be remembered for they did not falter during some of their darkest hours during World War II.

For likely errors in my story — and there may well be many — I crave indulgence.

I acknowledge help and encouragement from Jim Fyrth, author of *"The Signal Was Spain"* and co-editor of *"Women's Voices From The Spanish Civil War"*.

P. Fyvel

Part I

I Am Here

Chapter 1

Growing Up In Tottenham

A very early memory is of my mother pointing out the tiny house in an alley called Hale Gardens in which I was born on 24th April 1909. We were then living in Edith Road, only a stone's throw from the Gardens. The reason why we had moved was that my parents had fallen into arrears with the rent. Sometimes it was a question of "the moonlight flit". We were very poor. My father, known as "Punch" Phelps, but in fact a very kindly man, was a general labourer. He was frequently unemployed. Houses in Tottenham were mostly owned by private landlords and let to the working classes at low weekly rent. Little repair or redecoration was done and the neighbourhood had the air of a dilapidated slum.

When World War I came, my father was called to the Army while my mother worked in the local ammunitions factory. We were then six children in the family, five of us and Charlie Harris whom my mother had taken into our home without a legal adoption. I was the youngest but one. Soon food and other shortages began and we children often went about barefoot. We were frequently hungry and tended to hang about outside factory gates holding out our hands to emerging workers, hoping they would hand over remains of their sandwich lunch.

I remember the Zeppelins and bombs being dropped. One Zeppelin over Cuffley was caught in the searchlights and brought down in flames by a plane. The pilot gained a Victoria Cross which was recently sold by his niece. The crowds in the street cheered but I felt sorry for those being burnt alive. Trains, filled with wounded soldiers, began to arrive at Tottenham Railway Station, where fleets of ambulances took the casualties to North Middlesex Hospital in Edmonton.

One day, returning home from school, I noticed hustle and bustle in our house and several neighbours were present. My younger brother George had been born. I was shown a birthmark on his little bottom, believed in some way related to the Zeppelin which had been brought down a few nights before his birth. Soon the onus of looking after the new baby and the subsequent ones fell on me. My mother's hands were already full.

The war ended and my father returned. For him, again, came hard physical work, punctuated by periods of unemployment with queuing up every day outside the employment exchange in all sorts of weather waiting for any type of job that might be available. My father never beat us even when we children must have exasperated him in the extreme. He was popular in the neighbourhood as he had the gift of humorous repartee. He bore the indignities of poverty with stoicism and a cockney's resilience. It was only when he had a few pennies in his pocket and had been to the pub that he lost his affability. I have never liked pubs or other places devoted to alcohol and greatly deplore the 'lager lout' image of some of our young people.

My mother was small and wiry. In my mind's eye I carry a picture of her with jet-black plaited hair covered by a man's cloth cap, a white blouse and a long black ragged skirt, a coarse sacking tied round her waist in place of an apron, and wearing boots done up by means of side buttons and with a broom in her hand. Unlike my father she had outbursts of temper and bouts of depression, fortunately short-lived. However, she was not averse to beating us children when we undoubtedly deserved it. Sometimes, after we had been more troublesome than usual and my mother could no longer put up with it, she would stalk out of the house, shouting "I'm going to drown myself". We were frightened, because we knew of bodies being dragged out of the River Lea (which was not far away) and had seen the corpses being wheeled away to the mortuary. We would follow her, crying and whimpering like goslings behind the mother goose, until we eventually lost sight of her. After several hours my mother would return in a better frame of mind; she had perhaps gone to a friend and had a few drinks. Clearly the pressures then on working-class women, bringing up large families on little money without the household appliances and supermarkets of today, were immense. Being in debt, visits to the pawnshop, fogs and floods, mice and bugs, as well as frequent sickness amongst the children, were constant accompaniments of my mother's life.

When the twins, Reuben and Harry were born, a large
perambulator was bought on the never-never system. I trundled
through the streets of Tottenham, pushing this high, heavy pram
with the twins, one at each end, Georgie sitting in the middle and
Rosie at my side clinging to my dress. I began to miss school in
order that I might take the younger children to the Green, while
Mother did the housework. That is when I began to knit and
crochet, at which I became quite adept. I also helped her when she
took the babies to the welfare clinic.

My mother often needed me at home, especially on wash-days. It
took the whole day from morn till night to complete the family
wash, augmented by that from neighbours. I still retain memory of
the smell of soap-suds, the steamy atmosphere permeating
throughout the little house from the wash-tub in the scullery and
from the water in the copper kept boiling by a small fire; also the
hard work entailed in turning the iron handle of the old mangle.
The involuntary truancy from school led to serious gaps in my
education, especially in simple arithmetic.

When I was thirteen, my mother took me away from school so that
I should look for work. Youngsters had no difficulty in finding
employment at that time. I had quite a succession of jobs at local
factories, such as Lebus's, Gestetner's, Eagle Pencil and
Maynard's, making furniture, office equipment and sweets
respectively. However, after a fortnight or so, birth certificates of
the juvenile employees were required by the Factory Inspector and,
as I was below the statutory age of employment, I left before he
arrived. Nevertheless, I obtained useful insight into the
employment conditions of juvenile labour in factories and
workshops which, many years later, stood me in good stead in
placement of physically handicapped youths.

After the various short factory jobs, my mother sent me into
domestic service with a family in Tankerton, near Whitstable, on
the Thames Estuary. I liked the uniform and tiny bedroom at the
top of the house. However, it was the first time I had been
separated from my brothers and sisters; I felt terribly homesick and
wrote every day to my mother to take me away, which she
eventually did.

When fourteen years old, just after my baby sister Louisa was
born, I obtained a steady job. No doubt today the set-up would be
called a sweat-shop. The owner and a few girls worked in one small
room making dresses and costumes for the D'Oyly Carte Company
which performed the Gilbert and Sullivan operas at the Savoy

Theatre in the West End of London. The hours were long and the wages low, five shillings per week, but we had the satisfaction in seeing the end-product of our labour. I learnt and became quite skilled in dressmaking, sewing and embroidery which, because of failing sight I cannot enjoy today.

At Sunday School I came under the influence of the teachers and their families. I joined the Plymouth Brethren to which some of them belonged, became very earnest and adhered strictly to their precepts. We met, prayed and sang hymns in a little tin chapel in Broad Lane, Tottenham, where I believe it still stands today. I became very familiar with the Holy Scriptures and could recite long passages. My speech and accent improved. I dressed demurely, used no make-up, kept my hair long and stayed well away from dance-halls and cinemas, the places then giving some colour and glamour to the lives of working-class young people. At home I was nicknamed the "Bible-Puncher".

To compensate for some of my lost schooling I began to attend evening classes. One of the tutors, a Mr Turner, and his wife befriended me and discussed my future. When, as a child, I had been a patient in the Prince of Wales Hospital, I had felt drawn to the work of the nurses. Mr Turner encouraged me to try for a career in nursing and for this I am particularly grateful to him.

Chapter 2

Nursing

Application forms for entry into a School of Nursing required details of educational attainments and I had none. Furthermore, I had to state the occupation of my father. Thinking that 'general labourer' would prove a handicap I promoted him, as he sometimes worked for the Council, to "local government officer", but the ruse did not succeed, no hospital would look at me. I then wrote a letter to the Matron of the Eastern Fever Hospital in Homerton Grove, Hackney, appealing to her to grant me a personal interview which she did. As a result, the Matron accepted me for the two years' course of fever training. She told me that the other prospective student nurses were of higher educational standards and that I might find the training difficult. The year was 1927 and I was eighteen years old.

The Eastern Hospital was one of several hospitals in Greater London, called Fever or Isolation Hospitals, specialising in the treatment of infectious diseases such as diphtheria, scarlet fever, smallpox, erysipelas, cerebrospinal meningitis, whooping cough and measles. These were then still very rife in the population and affected particularly children. The Fever Hospitals were administered centrally by the London County Council and I believe the Chief Medical Officer of Health at County Hall was then Sir Frederick Menzies. Some sixty years on, the need for such Fever Hospitals has largely disappeared. The Eastern Hospital came to house the Institute of Dermatology and the In-Patient Department of St. John's Hospital for Diseases of the Skin for some years. Now the handsome prize-winning District Hospital for Hackney has been built on its site in Homerton.

The intake of new student nurses began their practical work on the wards immediately, while receiving lectures and theoretical

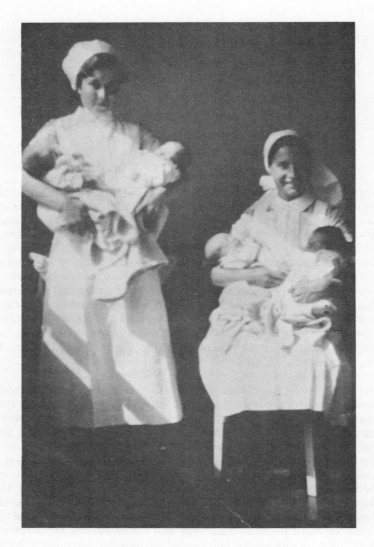

Nurse Penny Phelps (L) with a colleague

instruction from the Sister Tutor. We also had lectures from the medical staff. I took careful notes, kept my note-books and they accompanied me on subsequent assignments until I lost them in the Spanish Civil War. The sheet-anchor of the patients' treatment in those days was observation and good nursing which provided time for the natural bodily defences to overcome the infection. Few specific measures, other than diphtheria antitoxin, were then available, which was well before the advent of chemotherapeutic agents like M & B or antibiotics like penicillin. In lobar pneumonia, for example, we ensured that the temperature did not rise too high by tepid sponging or, conversely, after the crisis, that it did not fall too low by the use of the electric cradle or hot-water bottles. Often we heard the clanging bells of the ambulances warning the emergency ward of a case of croup needing an immediate tracheotomy. Then we had to watch the young patients very closely, as there was always the chance of the inner tube clogging with mucus which would cut off life-giving air. Toxins from diphtheria could produce serious effects on the heart muscle making movement or exertion on the part of the patients hazardous. We had to do everything for them and, when it became necessary, feed them through nasal tubes.

We nursed many patients suffering from typhoid fever acquired during the Croydon epidemic of that time. The source was eventually traced to a contaminated well. We saw these patients through the difficult phases of their illness only to find that some would relapse and have the symptoms of typhoid fever all over again.

From the nature of the diseases we were nursing, the work was hard. The hours were far longer than today; discipline, derived from the precepts of Florence Nightingale, was strict and incidentally the salary was pretty low, but in spite of this, I felt nursing to be a wonderful profession.

The Eastern Hospital had pleasant grounds which contrasted with the rather grim surroundings. There were two tennis-courts. I learnt to play, was soon quite good and became a member of the team engaged in competitions against other hospitals. At the end of the first year I took the hospital examination and the General Nursing Council (GNC) Preliminary Examination, which I passed.

At the end of the second year I obtained the GNC Certificate of Fever Trained Nurse. As I did well in the hospital examinations I was selected to represent the Eastern Hospital against the other Fever Hospitals in competition for the Nurses' Gold Medal.

Unfortunately, because of a mishap, I arrived late in the examination room; I did not have time to finish off the last question and missed the medal by four marks, having received higher marks than the medallist in the practical and oral examination.

On completion of my fever training, I decided to do General Nursing and for this I entered Charing Cross Hospital for a three-year course; one year being clipped off because of my fever certificate.

Charing Cross Hospital was a handsome building near the railway station, designed by Decimus Burton during the Regency Period. It was then a hospital depending for its upkeep on voluntary contributions. The House Governor, Lord Inman, I remember, was famous for his ability as fund raiser. We had students, the medical school being affiliated to London University. The wards were on the large open system, instituted by Florence Nightingale; when the new Charing Cross Hospital was built in Fulham after World War II, wards were designed to be smaller and to have fewer beds. I remember attractive tiled murals in the wards and believe these were taken to be incorporated in the new hospital.

A nurses' home had been built in England's Lane near Hampstead Heath and we were taken by coach to and from the hospital. The nurses frequently received theatre tickets and I was able to hear some of the Gilbert and Sullivan operas at the Savoy Theatre in the nearby Strand; I wondered whether any costumes worn by the cast had in part been made by me.

The new knowledge and skills I acquired in my general training lay particularly in the field of surgical nursing and the work of the operating-theatre. Surgical techniques and procedures for common operations were learnt so that correct instruments should be produced for the surgeon and in the precise order they were required.

At the end of three years I sat my Final Examinations to become a State Registered Nurse. Now I could obtain the post of Staff Nurse in any hospital or other positions where services of a trained nurse were required.

I joined a Nursing Agency which sent me to hospitals in London and the Home Counties when holidays or illness had created a temporary vacancy. This widened my experience, but also showed me that many of our hospitals and medical institutions were not of a high standard and that people were living in poverty in many other areas other than Tottenham and Hackney which I had known.

Chapter 3

Hillcroft College and
Interlude in Welwyn Garden City

While on a visit home to Tottenham two years after completion of general training in nursing, I looked up Mr Turner, my former teacher at evening classes. He told me about Hillcroft College, a residential college providing a one-year's course in academic subjects for working-class women, who had left school at an early age. On Mr Turner's advice, I sought an interview with the Principal, Miss Fanny Street and, as a result, she offered me a vacancy in the college. The local education authority, Middlesex County Council, gave me a grant; I also received a bursary donated by a benefactor, Marjorie Anderson, and these two funds paid the fees for the year.

Hillcroft College was founded in the 1920s by a few women enthusiasts from the field of education. They were helped by Mr Thomas Wall, a Quaker and philanthropist and a member of the well-known ice-cream and sausage-manufacturing firm. In 1933, when I became a student, Hillcroft was housed in a large Victorian mansion in Surbiton, within easy reach of London.

Miss Fanny Street was a distinguished educationalist. She had been Principal since the college's foundation when it was in Beckenham and was on the point of retiring when I entered. Her successor was Miss M. K. Ashby with whom I was to strike up a close and lasting friendship which endured until she died in her late eighties a few years ago. The tutors at Hillcroft were all university graduates. Most lived in and participated freely in the life of the students, sitting at their tables during meals and sharing in the extra-curricular activities.

We were a group of about thirty-five students, some of whom had been factory or office workers, local government employees, shop-girls, nurses and domestics; a cross-section of the occupations open to working-class women. A few had been unemployed; a sign

15

of the times. Before being admitted to Hillcroft, students should already have participated in some aspect of further education, say by attendance at evening classes. In fact, many of my fellow students already had some academic background, which made me in comparison feel a bit of an ignoramus.

We were given a choice of subjects and I selected social history, European history, English literature, psychology, machinery of government and geography. The tutors gave lectures and, the classes being small, there was scope for discussion of the topics covered. The lynch-pin of our studies was the well-stocked library. Until I entered Hillcroft, I had hardly read a book other than nursing manuals. Now I was spending several hours a day in the library immersed in books, endeavouring to absorb and master their contents. The plunge into the world of the intellect was a very traumatic experience. My total ignorance seemed unbridgeable. However, I must have been reasonably quick in the uptake. Soon I possessed a modicum of knowledge and understanding which served as a springboard for further development of my studies. Spirits and confidence rose and the course became an increasing source of satisfaction.

The students wrote essays based on the content of the lectures supplemented by reading. These were then marked by the tutors. In one essay on "What do you consider the sphere of state action?" I discussed issues which appear to exercise the minds of politicians and others just as much today. I wrote that "opinions vary considerably and widely, from communism to 'laissez-faire'; the one desiring the most, the other the least possible state interference and control". I concluded that "the state should by a minimum of wise legislation aim to secure the greatest possible happiness and contentment for all its citizens by providing opportunity for work and leisure, allowing everyone to progress along their own individual lines and culture".

At the end of the year, most students returned to their former work or occupation, but some went on to a full university education. One of my contemporaries became a don at the London School of Economics and as a result of her distinguished work, she received an honour, the OBE. I left Hillcroft with a much-changed, fuller and sharper outlook on life.

The middle thirties were bad years for England and for the rest of the world. The economy was in serious trouble and the number of unemployed had risen to unprecedented heights. At home, groups of disconsolate men were standing about on street corners waiting for jobs and better times. After Hillcroft, I spent 1934 to 1936 in Welwyn Garden City, Hertfordshire, helping Mrs Eulalie Heron with her young children and in between doing temporary nursing work in the neighbourhood.

Mr Tom Heron, tall, handsome and bearded, was head of Cresta Silks, a firm dealing in hand-block printed fabrics and materials of distinctive designs. He was interested in theology and philosophy, and wrote poetry. Mrs Heron, a history graduate, and a friend of Miss Ashby, was fond of music, literature and nature. There were four children. Patrick, the eldest, showed an early talent for painting. Later he attended the Slade School of Art and is now an established modern artist. His studio is in Zennor on the Cornish coast near St. Ives. Some of his paintings hang in the Tate Gallery of which he has been a trustee. He has written books on painting and art. He is a CBE and occasionally contributes to *The Times* in support of art and our heritage. Next was Michael who became a priest and is now a prior at Cockfosters. The daughter Joanna taught history and married Bernard Waites, a Director of Education for Westmorland. On his retirement they bought an old farmhouse near Kendal in Cumbria and looked after Mr and Mrs Heron in their later years. The youngest son Giles became an organic farmer in Yorkshire.

So, on and off for two years, I shared the well-ordered life of a middle-class family and was able to contrast it with the atmosphere of near-crisis and the hard physical circumstances surrounding so many working-class families, which I had experienced in my childhood.

The Heron parents went out of their way to encourage talent in their children. There were singsongs around the piano, readings from Dickens and other classics and country walks which were lessons in botany and ornithology. When the Herons had company, the conversation was on matters I had learnt about at Hillcroft and which I thought were confined to dusty academic books or university lectures.

Welwyn Garden City was the product of the ideas of Ebenezer Howard and was planned after World World I. From a central area of community buildings and shops, radiated tree-lined roads which had detached houses behind green swards on either side. A special location for factories and other industrial enterprises had been established. The Garden City concept was used in the planning of the New Towns created after World War II. Recently I travelled on a Green Line coach that wound its way through the lanes of Welwyn to Stevenage. Here were very many attractive houses, some small, others large, not far from factories in green-field sites which were giving work to the people, all built in recent decades. Surely this is a better blueprint for Britain than large housing estates, in big cities and often far from factories or shops, like the

B

Broadwater Farm Estate which I got to know as a sister lived there.

Last year my dear friend Mrs Heron died in her 95th year. Only a few days previously she had written me an eight-page letter in her immaculate hand telling of the happenings in her family, not only about the children, but also her grand and even great-grandchildren. Mrs Heron was buried in the country churchyard of Selside amidst the fells. I placed a sprig of wild flowers, which she had loved so much, in her grave. Tom Heron had died one year previously.

In 1936 the Spanish Civil War began. Deep emotions were stirred. Many volunteers from the United Kingdom as well as from other countries went to Spain to take part in the fighting on the Republican and on Franco's side. A committee whose members included Lord Farringdon and Lady Hastings was formed to organise medical aid for Republican Spain. Nursing in Spain had been mainly the province of nuns and most were with Franco, leaving the Republicans short of nurses. I, therefore, offered my services to the Spanish Medical Aid Committee and was interviewed by George Jeger, Leah Manning and others and accepted. Soon along with Mrs Molly Murphy and another nurse I was on my way. I had never been outside the Home Counties; now I was crossing the Channel, taking the train to Paris, and then on to Port Bou and the Spanish frontier. It all happened very quickly, one of my last nursing duties in Hertfordshire had been to attend to the Jarrow hunger marchers and their very sore and blistered feet. Now I was in Spain. There was a long wait on the crowded station at Port Bou. Suddenly the people became animated, gesticulating and pointing: 'Aviones'! I saw and heard nothing, but for me the war had begun. In Barcelona we reported at the "English Flat" from which Winifred Bates and her colleagues administered the affairs of the Spanish Medical Aid Committee. With two other nurses I was being sent to Albacete to the headquarters of the International Brigades which would assign us to our various units. When we attempted to board the train from Barcelona to Valencia, this was already crammed full with soldiers. We were only able to squeeze onto the train by abandoning most of our baggage, having been assured that the precious equipment provided for us would be sent on, but I never saw it again. As the train approached Valencia the sun was shining although it was middle of winter. We were travelling through a green countryside of orange groves. When the train turned inland the scenery became barren and desolate and it began to rain. We were heading towards Albacete.

Part II

The Spanish Civil War

Chapter 4

English Penny

In Albacete my two fellow nurses and I were assigned quarters in a dingy hotel. Our room was next to a lavatory where the stench was overpowering. On one occasion, returning from a walk, we saw a stranger leaving our room. He had gone through our belongings. Foreigners, especially women, were regarded with suspicion as possible spies or enemy agents, hence the search, in spite of the medical insignia on our sleeves and hats.

After a few days of waiting in Albacete I was asked to report to medical headquarters and was interviewed by a tall officer with a flowing black moustache wearing a sheepskin coat. This was Goryan, Chief of the Medical Services of the 15th International Brigade. The language of the Internationals varied, usually being German or French, but Goryan addressed me in perfect English "Comrade Phelps, have you operating-theatre experience?" I replied in the affirmative. "Good, I shall take you to a unit where you will be very busy." Early next morning he arrived in a small camouflaged staff car and we drove at speed along the main Valencia-Madrid highway. Later we left it for the greater safety of minor roads. The Fascists had launched a major offensive to cut the main road to the south-east of Madrid.

To those on the Republican side, Franco's troops were always 'the Fascists' and regarded as a bunch of reactionary generals commanding sections of the regular army, particularly Moors from North Africa, brutal indigenous Fascists and, especially in the air, German Nazis and Italian Blackshirts. The people of Republican Spain, with whom I had already identified, were resisting valiantly: Madrid had stood firm all winter. Although the city had been

19

bombed without mercy, its lifeline, the road from Valencia, remained open and supplies were reaching the beleaguered populace.

We arrived in a suburb of Madrid where a mobile surgical hospital was forming. The personnel was composed of many nationalities. One of the Spanish orderlies called me English Penny and that name stuck to me throughout my stay in Spain. Amongst our transport of lorries and ambulances were special vans, called autochirs, presented by the American Medical Aid Organisation, which carried most of our surgical equipment, the operating-tables, electric generators, special lighting, sterilizers, metal boxes containing complete sets of surgical instruments for different kinds of operations, sterile gloves, gowns and linen — all brand-new.

Tired and dishevelled dispatch-riders arrived from the front with messages for Goryan. It was time to move off. So as not to attract enemy aircraft, our fully-laden convoy departed after dark. In the morning we passed through a village with a damaged church spire. Apparently, someone had fired from the spire on Republican soldiers gathered in the square below and had to be dislodged by gun-fire.

In the afternoon we arrived at Tarancón, a small town on the Madrid-Valencia road, at that time the railhead for goods arriving for the Republican army from the coast. The sound of gun-fire, though at a distance, indicated that fighting was going on. Aeroplanes in the sky were too high for us to recognise their markings whether they be Franco's or the Republicans'; an occasional thud of bombs could be heard.

We hurried to open up the hospital in a small school; three operating-tables were placed in a room on the ground floor and rows of stretchers were arranged in the corridors and elsewhere to accommodate the casualties on whom we would operate. Soon ambulances were bringing in the wounded, their injuries covered by field dresings and with a large 'M + ' marked on the forehead of those who had been injected with morphine and anti-tetanus serum. Many were in a parlous condition and clearly dying; some were already dead, but others were selected for immediate operation, while those regarded as minor casualties could await evacuation. Harry Evans, the English electrician, had fixed-up the lights. The sterilizers were on, sets of instruments for trephining the skull, amputating limbs and exploring chest and abdominal injuries were ready.

Soon we were hard at work. I assisted Dr Douglas Jolly, a New Zealander, and realised he was the best surgeon with whom I had ever been associated. He operated swiftly and dexterously however complicated the situation. We began in the late afternoon, continued throughout the night and all the following day until, in the evening, a lull in the flow of wounded, brought us to a temporary halt. Shrapnel and bullets were removed from body or skull, bleeding was staunched, lacerations were sutured and internal organs repaired. Shattered limbs were splinted, encased in plaster or amputated. My own duties kept on mounting. Soon I was anaesthetizing the wounded with ether or chloroform (in England I had seen so many anaesthetics given that I was quite familiar with the techniques) and handing over the face mask to an orderly as soon as the patient was under. I then scrubbed up and proceeded to assist the surgeon. As the operation neared its end, I gathered up the instruments and gave them to women helpers from the neighbourhood for cleaning. The instruments were then reassembled, placed in their appropriate metal containers and given to the attendant responsible for resterilizing the sets.

Immediately a wounded soldier was removed from the operating-table another waiting casualty was brought in. Fresh instruments were set out and the next operation began. Soiled linen was taken away by the local women to be washed, and when the clean laundry was returned it was sterilized. There was never enough linen so that we had to obtain some from the civilian population.

As more and more casualties arrived our pace quickened accordingly. Sometimes I found myself assisting at all three tables when my two nurse colleagues required rest pauses. For resuscitation we used mainly infusions of intravenous saline. Often veins were so collapsed that it was necessary to give the fluid intramuscularly. Blood transfusions were reserved for the most needy. A Canadian, Dr Norman Bethune, was in charge of the blood transfusion services for the International Brigades. He utilized the technique of storing blood on ice, developed by the Catalan surgeon Frederic Durán-Jorda. There was never time for cross-matching and we had to rely on precious supplies of universal-donor blood. Dr Bethune later went to China to join the Communist forces. He became a legendary figure as organiser of medical services and as a skilled surgeon. A book has been written about Dr Bethune entitled, *"The Scalpel, the Sword"*, and a university in China has been named after him.

To return to Tarancón and the continuous stream of casualties. For five days and nights we had only brief snatches of sleep and that on blood-soaked stretchers not occupied by the wounded. We were sustained by mugs of black coffee, bully-beef sandwiches and cigarettes. I had begun to smoke as did all other colleagues, male and female.

When fighting had eased up a little and casualties ceased arriving, our trials were not yet over: we heard the drone of aeroplanes, then the sound of heavy explosions and anguished cries. Bombs had fallen in the town, civilians were hurt and our work started all over again. The town's electricity failed as did our generator and we were operating by the light of torches. However, Evans struggled hard and restored the generator for which we were most grateful.

At last, no casualty was waiting and I took the opportunity for a stroll to the town square. On one side was a small cafe and I joined members of our unit sitting at the tables. On the other side was a petrol station, where lorries were refuelling. Suddenly there was an enormous explosion and a sheet of flame rose to the sky. The petrol station had received a direct hit and the carnage was horrific. I saw a small child and ran to pick it up. It was a girl; she was badly injured and one leg was obviously shattered. I stumbled with her in my arms to our hospital where Dr Jolly amputated the damaged limb. It was an incident I can never forget.

Another time during a lull I visited the English Medical Unit, commanded by Dr Alex Tudor Hart and stationed not far away. Some letters from home were waiting, but I remember most the good food and the smell of English cigarettes.

On my return Goryan told me I was to join a new mobile hospital nearer the front to cope with casualties from the fighting at the Jarama river.

Chapter 5

Valley of the Jarama

A rough stone building rather like a barn, standing in a small dell surrounded by trees between the towns of Chinchón and Perales, was converted into a "first hospital of evacuation". This was its official name. Conditions were primitive; we were without heating, electricity or running water. Trucks brought drinking water from a distance and its quality was suspect. A young American, Dr Robbins, arrived to attend to the sterilization of the water supply; even so, there was much tummy upset amongst us.

The International Brigades bore the brunt of the battle of the Jarama river. The battalions of the Brigades belonged to many nationalities. The men were volunteers who had gone to the Republicans' aid for various reasons; some were communists or had left-wing sympathies, others were of working-class origins who felt kinship with the Spanish workers; there were those whose motivation was anti-Fascism, because they might have experienced Fascism in their native country, some were humanitarians or idealists and a few were pure adventurers. There were even misfits from civilian life who were seeking an escape in fighting. Very few had been professional soldiers or had previous experience of military service.

In the battle of the Jarama, the International Brigades suffered very heavy casualties. Franco's troops were mainly regular soldiers from North Africa and included Moorish units. They established bridgeheads over the river and gained a foothold. However, they failed in their main objective of cutting the highway to Madrid. The British battalion of the 15th International Brigade was heavily engaged. The commander, Tom Wintringham, was wounded but not severely; he passed through our hospital and was then evacuated down the line.

Our unit was only a short distance behind the front line and the

23

fighting. We faced grim circumstances. The surgeons were mostly Spanish and, although skilful, they were not like Dr Jolly whose inspiration and boost to morale I missed very much. As at Tarancón, the very many casualties meant operating sessions that went on and on. We had insufficient staff to work any sort of shift system. It was the middle of February and the weather was bitterly cold, icy winds swept through the hospital making sleep difficult, especially as our beds consisted of blood-soaked frozen stretchers. The main threat hanging over our work was always that we would run out of essential medical supplies, such as needles, sutures, bandages, dressings and anaesthetics. During a comparative lull I went with an ambulance into Madrid to replenish the stocks. On our return journey, the ambulance was preceeded by a dispatch-rider. When we were approaching the Arganda bridge over the Jarama, the motor-cyclist suddenly wobbled and fell. We heard the rat-tat-tat of machine-gun fire. The driver of the ambulance, Izzy Kupchick, possibly from the East-End of London, put his foot down hard on the accelerator; we reached the bridge and sped across into safety. The main road had come within range of the enemy's forward position. However, our troops counter-attacked, regained the ground and traffic to and from Madrid proceeded safely once more. The body of the dead dispatch-rider was later recovered. Izzy Kupchick was later killed when his ambulance was hit by a shell.

On another occasion, during a quiet spell, Ted Fletcher, one of our ambulance drivers, took me and another nurse into the lines of the British battalion. We met the handsome and legendary Captain Nathan in his smart uniform and carrying a gold-tipped swagger-cane. In spite of the bad time they were having, the officers and men appeared cheerful and optimistic.

Gradually the fighting at the Jarama lessened. For our surgical teams the respite came in the nick of time. Through the sheer volume of work and its intensity under adverse conditions we were at the end of our tether. Perhaps also the Moors had been close enough for us to see in our imagination the glint of their bayonets.

> "There's a valley in Spain called Jarama,
> It's a place that we all know so well,
> For 'tis there that we gave of our manhood,
> And most of our dear comrades fell."

was sung by our troops to the tune of the "Red River Valley".

Our surgical unit was pulled back to Tarancón for regrouping. It was March and a new active front had opened to the north, in the area of the Guadalajara river. The Nationalists were attacking and their forces were mainly Italians. However, they were defeated by their Italian compatriots, the Garibaldis of the International Brigade. The Nationalist forces retreated in haste leaving much equipment including medical supplies. Our hospital had moved to this sector and we were overjoyed to receive the unexpected bounty which was immediately put to good use. Many wounded Italian prisoners came under our care. They were not Fascist bully-boys, but young conscripts from the Italian countryside. They seemed perplexed as to why they were in Spain and frightened by the fate they imagined would befall them. I remember an Italian boy, whose jaw had been shot away exposing the gullet. We did our best to get food into him. He could not speak, but I felt he was expressing gratitude with his eyes for our efforts to help and make him comfortable.

We were not long on the Guadalajara front before the unit was moved again, this time to the small town of Colmenar Viejo in the valley of the Jarama river which is to the north of Madrid. There was little military activity now, but we were busy acting as field hospital to the troops and the local civilians. Here I teamed up with Una Wilson, a tall, blonde Australian and May MacFarlane, a small, wiry, dark-haired New Zealander with tortoise-shell rimmed glasses. They were experienced nurses, who had been through hard times on another front, and both were pleased to have me work with them. Goryan had been promoted to chief of the 15th Medical Division, and Dr Max Langer, an Austrian, was now head of the Medical Services of the 15th International Brigade which included the British battalion. He had been in a concentration camp and suffered a great deal at the hands of the Germans. One of the surgeons was Renée Dumont, a smiling, good-looking Belgian, fond of music, languages and popular with everyone. He was not a communist and came to Spain on humanitarian grounds. He and I visited outlying units riding a horse called Abraham. I would be at the back of Dr Dumont holding him firmly round his waist, just like one sees on the films. One day I decided that I would ride Abraham by myself but, when I mounted him, he suddenly turned and started galloping towards the Fascist lines. I pulled hard on the reins to turn him round when he reared up with his back legs, threw me over his head and galloped back to our post. I got up, my mouth full of dust and gravel, and began a weary journey back to the unit. In the distance I espied a group coming towards me with a stretcher; they had seen Abraham return riderless.

Two weeks after we came to Colmenar I began to feel unwell, suffering from headaches and fatigue, and put this down to the overwork and poor food of the month before, when the front had been very active. Dr Dumont diagnosed the "grippe" and sent me to bed. Another two days passed and I felt very ill and seemed not to be fully aware of my surroundings. Later I was told that a Spanish guard had found me wandering outside the compound, delirious and in my bare feet. I had typhoid fever. Una Wilson and May MacFarlane took it in turns to nurse me and thanks to them I pulled through, even though the story had spread that I was dead. No, not yet. There was a kick in me still. Lady Hastings from the Spanish Medical Aid Committee visited me and suggested I return to England to regain strength, and also to raise money for Spain.

It was early summer 1937 and coronation time for King George VI. The country was still not awake to the dangers from the dictators. The government of Neville Chamberlain was pursuing a policy of non-intervention in the Spanish Civil War. I spoke at several meetings in London and the provinces. These were organised mainly by the Labour Party or other left-wing groups, but sometimes contrary views were expressed. At one meeting a heckler cried "But Spain is red". "Yes", I replied, "red with blood, the blood is spattered over the streets and the gutters often run with it. For weeks my arms were splashed with blood". I had not envisaged a role as a public speaker and propagandist nor that I could become emotional about things, but usually a tangible result to my efforts ensued in the form of gifts or money for Spanish Medical Aid. I returned to Colmenar with brand-new instruments. These were soon to be used at the Battle of Brunete.

Chapter 6

Friends Die at Brunete

On my return journey, Barcelona still looked gay in bright summer sunshine, but in Valencia and all the way up the road to Madrid were signs of enemy aerial bombardment. At Colmenar Viejo, the personnel of my unit looked more relaxed and rested. Fighting had been mainly up in the North where the Guernica horror had been perpetrated. Bilbao had fallen, Santander was under attack and Basque refugee children were being sent to England. The Madrid front, however, had been quiet but there were rumours of fresh battles and this time the Republicans would be on the offensive. Our hospital had undergone some changes. Langer was still chief and Dumont, senior surgeon, but Dr Ronald Sollenberger, a big man with a jet-black beard would be up at the front with the casualty collecting post. Dr Groseph, a chubby little Austrian, who knew little Spanish or English, was a general duties officer as was Pierre, supposedly a close relative of Coty, the French perfume millionaire. At any rate, the room he shared was always cluttered up with bottles of scent. Dr Seymour Robbins, the light-hearted American responsible for water purification, was now permanently attached to us. A few young Englishmen had come as ambulance drivers. Una Wilson had been ill and was gone, but little May MacFarlane was still with the unit. So this time we two would work together.

We moved off in convoy one warm July night through the eerily-deserted streets of Madrid and arrived about midday in Hoya de Manzanares, one of Madrid's smartest summer resorts. It had large villas with gardens full of flowers. The surrounding green fields were bathed in sunshine. The air was invigorating, its freshness derived from the snow-capped sierras not far away. And we were to have another wonderful surprise. Our quarters proved to be in a

27

marvellous modern sanatorium with large bright rooms, beautifully tiled floors, black and green marbled bathrooms and a fine garden all around. Our good fortune was short-lived, but I will never forget the beauty of Hoya de Manzanares. We soon moved south towards the front and set up the hospital in a large house called La Solana at Torrelodones, between two hills and at the junction of the roads leading from Madrid to the King's Palace of El Escorial and to Brunete. At the top of La Solana was a tiny room with space for two camp-beds. May MacFarlane and I took it for ourselves. This time we would not sleep on blood-sodden stretchers.

On the evening and night of 5th July 1937, the combat troops quietly tramped past our building singing softly while they marched. The different battalions of the International Brigades, including the British, sang their own national songs. While hoping for victory, I had to ask myself what would happen to all these men and how many casualties would be the outcome.

I cleaned and prepared the operating-theatre while May attended to the sterilizers. Suddenly, before the battle had even begun, the first casualties arrived. These were Spanish children from Torrelodones. They had found some hand-grenades which had exploded. One child had facial injuries, and in another both hands had been blown off. The horrible injuries would be their memories of the Spanish Civil War. While we were still operating on the children, the sun rose and the guns opened up. Our attack had begun. By noon ambulances could no longer enter the yard of La Solana. It was full of the wounded on stretchers. Although our organisation was better than on the Jarama, some casualties were already dead before we could do anything for them.

We again worked day and night. However, this time May MacFarlane and I, along with Spanish nurses, were on a shift system. We now had heat and flies instead of the cold to contend with. The atmosphere in the operating-theatre was stifling and the floor slippery with caked blood. But still the news was good, our troops had taken Villanueva de la Canada, a large village some miles away. Then they stormed the town of Brunete and advanced still further. The Fascist army, however, rushed up fresh troops and the fighting, with our men stripped to the waist, raged day after day over the same few kilometres of ground.

Knowing the destruction of our hospital would demoralise our side, Franco's German and Italian aerial friends were always trying for a direct hit. In the little room at the top of the hospital building walls and ceilings trembled with every near miss, until one day the ceiling came down on May's camp-bed. Luckily she was not in it, but after that we slept in the open in an adjacent field.

Some nine or ten days later our attack had been halted and our soldiers dug in to consolidate their gain. Then came the Fascist counter-attack and with the weight of armour, planes and big guns against us, Brunete was lost, but our soldiers resisted every subsequent attack day after day. In the operating-theatre the flow of casualties and the heat and flies continued unremittingly. As had occurred on the Jarama front, we became desperately short of supplies. Ether and chloroform ran out and Novocaine, Evipan or spinal anaesthesia was used. When we were without gowns, I draped the surgeon in sheets given to us by the civilians. Once we were plunged into semi-darkness — the mains had failed as did our over-worked generator, which it had done before in similar circumstances. Three operations were in progress at the time and the surgeons had to make do with the light of torches and the reflection from the fires burning in nearby Villanueva de la Canada.

The last days of battle brought terrible losses. A casualty was carried into the operating-theatre. A weak voice said "Penny, don't you know me?" I had a fearful shock. It was George Nathan, now a major commanding a regiment. He was in great pain. I gave him an injection, put the anaesthestic mask on his face and we began to operate. A piece of shrapnel had pierced the liver, diaphragm and lungs and had lodged in the spine. It was quite hopeless. After the operation we took Nathan upstairs. I stayed with him having given an intramuscular saline infusion and repacked his wounds. Our best officer was dying. Later Jock Cunningham, commander of the British Battalion, came over and Nathan's body was taken away for a special military funeral.

The next day I took a quick ride to Hoya de Manzanares to try and replenish medical stocks. On my return I met Langer and knew from the expression on his face that something very serious had happened. Because of a temporary lull in the flow of casualties, a group from the hospital had gone forward to visit and cheer up the troops at the front, and while they were at the collecting post it suffered a direct hit from a bomb. Dr Sollenberger, Dr Groseph, Dr Seymour Robbins, Pierre, and many others of our ablest men who had become my personal friends had all been killed. We who remained were devastated.

At last the Fascist counter-offensive was slackening. The remnants of the British battalion were moved out of the line and passed through Torrelodones. For days they had fought in the torrid heat and they were utterly exhausted. I had a small supply of English tea, condensed milk and sugar; I prepared a large jug of tea and poured it out for the men as they wearily marched past our hospital. Possibly, a few men are alive today who remember their unexpected mug of tea of over fifty years ago.

Chapter 7

Journey Through a Spanish Night

The 15th International Brigade which included the British Battalion and our mobile hospital, was withdrawn from the front to recuperate and reorganise. The lines of the front had been advanced, though only a short distance, but enough to give a feeling of success to the Republican army's recent campaign. I went for a while to the "English Villa", situated on the beach at Valencia not far from the port. A young English girl, Sybil Clarke, was in charge whom I liked very much. English nurses could stay there while resting or passing through Valencia. Goryan came over on a visit. He was now a high-up in the army's medical hierarchy. He proposed I go home on a short leave. It might help to lessen the blow of the events in which so many of my colleagues had been killed.

In England the summer was fine and sunny. I saw my family and friends and spoke at meetings on behalf of Spanish Medical Aid. After Brunete, where so many of our soldiers had fallen, I was able to impart a sense of urgency to my appeals and to arouse support and even enthusiasm. However, the country as a whole was still indifferent to what was happening in Spain and I was dismayed to hear of Fascist or pro-Fascist factions at home. The English newspapers carried the news: "Five Italian seaplanes raid Valencia, sixty casualties". "Night-raid on Barcelona. Many killed". Alicante, Gandia, Tarragona, Gijon, Tortosa — all were bombed. Some three years later it was London, Coventry, Liverpool, Glasgow, Birmingham and other cities which suffered. In 1937, however, only the Spanish people bore these tribulations.

Soon I was returning to Spain along with others in an ambulance. At the frontier a Scandinavian officer poked amongst our medical supplies with a stick. He was enforcing "non-intervention" and looking for concealed weapons. Barcelona now looked grim. Many houses, whole blocks, were in ruins from the bombing. Food was terribly expensive and the shops were almost empty. I could not find the delicious little sweets I had enjoyed on previous visits.

In Valencia a conference of women was being held. I represented English nurses and May MacFarlane, New Zealand. We met La Passionaria, the famous Spanish Revolutionary Women's Leader, whose beautiful speaking voice and manner were very impressive. Everyone was still optimistic and in the parks and gardens flowers were blooming in the sunshine, even among bomb-damaged buildings. However, when May and I were on the train to Albacete to report back to headquarters, we soon gathered that things were not going well. Santander had fallen and the Asturian miners were cut off in a small stretch of wild country round Oviedo. Nor had the Republican offensive on the Aragon front been successful.

Langer was now chief medical organiser in Albacete. We arrived after midnight but he was still in his office and while we talked the telephone kept ringing and people were continually popping in. An epidemic of typhoid was rampant on the Aragon front. A call had come from the Garibaldi Battalion, stationed at their base in Quintanar de la Republica fifty kilometres away, to say there was scarlet fever in the unit and asking for a doctor as their own had gone down with it.

The British Battalion was stationed not far from Quintanar at Tarazona, and the Thaelmann and Franco-Belgian battalions were also nearby. At any moment these units were destined to return to the front. The Garibaldis would have to be isolated in order to prevent spread of the scarlet fever epidemic and their sick also needed attention. No medical officer was available, however.

"Thank God you have arrived Penny" Langer said as he greeted me. "You are fever-trained, aren't you?"

"I had plenty of fever experience in England", I replied.

"Right! I will send you as a temporary medical officer to the Garibaldis until I can obtain a doctor. You will go now; in an hour, in half an hour!"

It all sounded rather crazy to me, nor could May MacFarlane accompany me as she was needed elsewhere. Langer set-to at once preparing papers giving me full authority to take all measures to bring the epidemic under control, arranging an ambulance, medical supplies, and money, and promising to send an interpreter in the morning. "I shall rely on you Penny, to control the epidemic. It must not spread — you know what that would mean," Langer said as, in spite of my misgivings, he saw me off in an ambulance (which was pretty old and falling to bits).

With a young American driver I set off into the complete darkness of the night. It was raining hard. When eventually we arrived at our destination, I slipped on the muddy ground. We had stopped in front of a big building which proved to be the hospital for the military and civilians of Quintanar.

After hammering on the heavy door we were finally admitted by a scruffy, sleepy figure purporting to be both guard and night orderly. As I turned on the light in the ward, I saw rows of beds in which men half-asleep were turning, cursing, and grunting. The first patient who caught my attention was clearly very ill, most likely a typhoid case, I thought, and one that should never be in an open ward, but isolated and preferably at a special hospital. The men's heads were resting on bundles of their clothes as they had no pillows. The floor was littered with pieces of bread, and half-empty glasses of wine were at their bedside. Chamber-pots under the beds were full. All windows appeared shut and the stench was awful.

The man I suspected of having typhoid fever was in a critical condition. His temperature was clearly raised and his pulse was feeble. Yet he had no temperature chart by his bed. As I looked around I thought of lice — a whole army of them must be in this room. How was everything to be cleaned up? A start must be made! It was growing light and I had been travelling the whole of the previous day and through the night but the job had to be tackled there and then. First, the ill patient must be isolated. I told the guard to fetch and heat up some water. He objected. The door, he said, he had to guard the door. Because of the Fascists! I felt like knocking him on the head with his rifle. In my poor Spanish I explained the camerado was very ill, "Muy mal. Mal tifus!" I found a room upstairs where orderlies were sleeping and noticed a vacant bed. Downstairs was a small consulting room with a dirty old couch. This was removed and the bed from upstairs brought down and installed in the now vacant room by the reluctant guard and the American ambulance driver. Returning to the sick patient, I stripped off his shirt and underwear infested with lice and soiled with faeces, plunged the clothes (later to be burnt) in strong disinfectant and proceeded to sponge him down. I made him comfortable, put him into a clean shirt and then had him transferred to the newly made-up bed in the consulting room. A large notice "No entrada" was put up on the door of what had become the isolation room.

It was now seven o'clock in the morning and an interpreter had arrived from Albacete. The unit's Italian Commandante was away and with the interpreter I went to see his deputy who had just finished breakfast. He showed no sign of surprise at seeing a woman. I explained that to combat the epidemic of scarlet fever and other infections, drastic measures would have to be taken. All leave was to be cancelled, no soldier was to leave Quintanar. Sentries were to be posted immediately to see that order was enforced. The medical orderlies of all companies were to come for instructions. The case of suspected typhoid would have to be reported to headquarters at once. I wished to see all the cooks who henceforth would have to be particularly scrupulous in washing their hands. No men with sore throats or rashes should come to the hospital, instead I would see them in their quarters. The drinking water was to be tested. With his permission I would inspect barracks, kitchens, dining-rooms and the men's utensils and the latrines. I hoped he would co-operate in all this as it was important. The vice-commandante was very polite saying si, si, but he goggled a little at my many requests. I left him and returned to the hospital accompanied by the interpreter.

Chapter 8

A Doctor for the Garibaldis

A group of soldiers had gathered at the entrance to the hospital on hearing that a doctor had arrived. They were reporting sick but none was really ill. I called the medical orderlies together and informed them of a new rule, the sick of each company would have to report to the hospital at separate times. Then I made a round of the barracks. The troops' quarters were dirty, overcrowded two-storey barns. The bunks, eating and drinking utensils were all in a sorry state. I spoke to the cooks, explained how typhoid was carried from hand to mouth and that absolute cleanliness should be the watchword.

I discovered cesspools not properly covered over and ordered that they be attended to immediately. When the tour of inspection was completed, I went into the village where the so-called Spanish Company of Workers was stationed. They consisted of handymen who were responsible for upkeep of the base. I explained to their Commander that to eradicate the epidemic the dwellings and sleeping quarters would have to be fumigated and all clothing and personal belongings disinfected. To get started, fresh accommodation for one whole company would be required. He thought for a while and then said that one of Quintanar's three churches was empty and not used. He took me to the church. Clearly it would make ideal temporary accommodation for one whole company and I had no qualms about putting it to that use. If his men could knock up the required number of bunks, I would obtain palliasses from Albacete. What about baths? He said that only a few soldiers turned up for showers as the water was ice-cold. I requested that hot showers be fixed up by however temporary an arrangement so that by the next day, during disinfection, every man would be able to have a hot shower.

With her staff at Quintanar

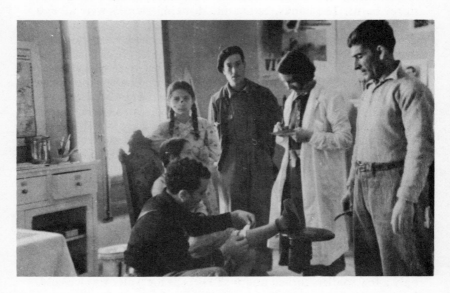

At work

On return to the hospital, I sat down by the telephone to get through to Albacete. At last I was speaking to Langer. I reported the typhoid case and then put in a request for palliasses, medical supplies, boots, mugs, plates, cutlery and other requirements and made arrangements for the disinfecting and delousing van to come the next day. When I finished on the telephone I realised that I was ravenously hungry. I had a scrap meal and sipped some sweet clinging wine. I felt it warm me inside and had time to reflect that it was strange to be alone, a woman from England, amongst Italian men in a Spanish village miles from anywhere. However, there was little time for idle thoughts. I began to write-up reports of actions so far, but was interrupted by the arrival of two children from the village. The first was suffering from burns and these I dressed, while the other had broken his arm. I put this in splints, stopped a passing car and asked the driver if he would take the child to the civilian hospital in Albacete with a note explaining that he was from Quintanar where there was an outbreak of scarlet fever. Then I returned to the hospital to deal with the patients already there. With the help of the interpreter I made a complete round, noting name, age, date of admission and what company he belonged to and started them on temperature charts. Some men were fit enough to be discharged and I gave them a note on which date they were to return to full duty. A record of the sick in hospital was prepared for the Commandante. Then there was still time to have the ward cleaned and put in order. The hospital stores, I discovered, were really quite well stocked and fresh linen, blankets and shirts could be issued, while pillows were noted as an item to be ordered from Albacete. In a small room upstairs was a cupboard in which I could lock up essential medicines and other materials.

It was now two o'clock in the morning and I prepared to go to bed, twenty-four hours or so after leaving Albacete and Langer and May MacFarlane. As I closed my eyes I became violently sick. The vomiting over, I felt much better and at once sank into a deep sleep.

I woke in the morning to thoughts of what now had to be done. Before breakfast, I was on the telephone again to Albacete making arrangements for the day and the removal of the typhoid patient. Then off to the church which had been already swept and cleaned. Double wooden bunks, hastily knocked together by the handymen, had been put up. During the morning lorries arrived from Albacete with straw palliasses and additional bedding. Temporary hot showers had been installed and the sterilising and delousing van had arrived and was ready. The men of one company were assembled; they were stripped, leaving boots, belts and other

leather articles in one corner, clothes in a second and their personal
belongings, done up in marked bundles, in a third corner of the
barn. These personal belongings were collected and disinfected.
Meanwhile the men entered the showers and were thoroughly
scrubbed down. Any sores or cuts were noted by the orderlies.
Then, wearing only a towel round their middles, they filed in
batches of five into my room to be examined. Some were self-
conscious but their was no time for false modesty. I inspected their
tongues, throats and skin for rashes and found three suspects of
scarlet fever who were immediately isolated. As each batch of
soldiers passed through, they were issued with fresh uniforms,
clean shirts, vests, pants, socks and footwear.

After this, under strict instructions not to mix with men from
other companies, they marched into their new quarters in the
church where they remained until their barracks had been fully
fumigated.

The following morning, the former barracks of this company were
sealed. The fumigating gang from Albacete then performed their
job thoroughly; the smell of disinfectant was so strong it hung
about the place for days. The treated barracks were then cleaned
from top to bottom and given back to the troops who had been
quartered in the church. Each subsequent day was a repetition of
the first until the entire battalion of 600 men, including the officers,
had passed through the disinfecting process and were installed in
their newly-cleaned quarters.

While this went on, I was busy at the hospital looking after about
forty patients with my staff of army orderlies including a few
women and girls from the village. At first we had about half a
dozen fresh cases of scarlet fever a day. These were evacuated by
special ambulance to the isolation hospital at Villanueva in charge
of Dr Van Reamst, who had belonged to our unit at Brunete. Less
than three weeks later, no fresh cases occurred, the epidemic of
scarlet fever had ended. It had been necessary to be strict and to
issue many orders. When Langer visited and saw the change that
had taken place in the hospital he was amazed. I felt the purpose of
sending me to Quintanar had been achieved and wanted to return
to duties as nurse with a surgical unit but, the front being quiet,
Langer wanted me to stay. My reward, however, was being given
the rank of honorary medical officer. Now I was Lieutenant Penny
Phelps of the Spanish Republican Army, medical officer to the
Garibaldi Battalion of the 15th International Brigade. Luckily,
about two months later, the Republican Government de-militarised
all women and I gladly returned to being a nurse. However, Silvo

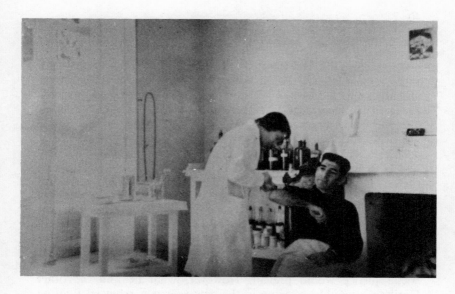

Giving an inoculation

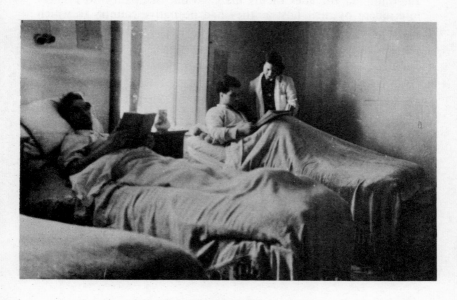

Ward round

Morelli, the tall, serious Commandante, still insisted that I take my meals in the Officers' Mess.

The Garibaldi Battalion was a small unit of the 15th International Brigade. These few hundred anti-Fascist Italians were already famous for their fighting qualities, especially when they defeated much larger Italian forces on Franco's side at Guadalajara. They were a remarkable body of men. In their khaki uniforms and with a red scarf wound round the neck they looked dashing and picturesque. Most had suffered for their ideals and had been in prison and concentration camps in Italy. In spite of their determination they bore a light-hearted air. They were as patriotic about their native Italy as they were anti-Fascist in sentiment.

The political commissar of the battalion was Roberto Vincenzi. He was very good looking, spoke fluent Spanish, French and some English. Roberto and I when work was slack, often went for long walks in which he talked to me earnestly about the new world where social justice would prevail. However, what he and the other Garibaldis would be facing in the new year was renewed fighting against increasingly heavy odds and, when the remnants of the International Brigades finally marched out of Spain into France, internment by their host as they had no native country to which they could return.

Chapter 9

The Garibaldis Leave Quintanar

There was plenty of work for me. After months of intense fighting at the front many Garibaldis were ailing and my small hospital was kept busy. The soldiers came to me when pieces of shrapnel or slithers of dead bone were working to the surface. I would then remove the foreign body under local anaesthetic or use ethyl chloride spray. I regularly inspected the barracks, kitchens and dining areas and, as I passed through, the soldiers held out their drinking mugs, plates and cutlery for inspection. I had to ensure that sanitary arrangements remained good, and that the hot showers, at first considered as only temporary, continued in working order. One day Langer brought General Rojo, who was Chief of Staff of the Republican Army, on a tour of inspection. They went right through the base and the General told me of his satisfaction at what he had seen of the medical and sanitary arrangements.

After my first typhoid patient had been transferred to Albacete, where, poor fellow, he died, other cases cropped up both among the troops and also the civilians. Langer decided the whole population of the village, both civil and military, would have to be inoculated with TAB vaccine. The civilians were first and the laborious operation, which fell upon me and my orderlies, went smoothly. Then it was the turn of the soldiers. Not all came for their first injection, still fewer for the second, in fact, almost none. They had a prejudice against inoculations and disliked the tiny needle prick. I lectured them, threatening to report their behaviour to headquarters, informing them of how on the Aragon front men had gone down with typhoid like flies and, if care was not taken, our battalion would become a liability, not an asset, to the Spanish Republican Army. This worked and over the following days the

41

men received their vaccines. After the soldiers, it was the turn of the officers. However, they refused to come and dismissed the inoculations as a matter of no consequence. This was a defeat I could not readily accept. One evening I took a tray with the necessary materials for injections to the Officers' Mess and left a guard on the door with instructions to lock it at my signal. When, at the end of the meal, I produced the tray, the officers made a dash for the now locked door like a pack of schoolboys. Thereupon I warned them about the consequences of disobeying higher command orders. They began laughing, thinking I was joking, but, in fact, I was angry with them. However, after further persuasion from the Political Commissar, Roberto Vincenzi, the officers finally plucked up courage and received their TAB vaccine.

I had some difficult cases of malingering. I remember one man who came hobbling on sticks because he could not bend his knee. When I tried to flex it, he restrained me immediately, complaining it was too painful. So I put him on a couch and gave him a light whiff of anaesthetic. At once his leg became limp and his knee could be easily flexed. When he opened his eyes and spoke (a minute or so later) I told him that he could get up and leave. He reached for his sticks. "No sticks", I exclaimed. He, the one-time invalid, then walked out clapping his hands in joy as he passed those soldiers who were waiting to see me — a miracle had been performed!

On another occasion a medical orderly from Tarazona, where the British were stationed, called on the telephone. Two lorries had collided and a German soldier from the Thaelmann Battalion had been hurt. One arm was badly lacerated and some of his fingers crushed. Their doctor was away and my advice was sought. I suggested they contact the medical centre at Albacete, meanwhile give the injured man morphine and anti-tetanus injection and keep him warm. Soon they were on the telephone again. They could not move the man because he was in too much pain to undertake the long journey to Albacete. There was nothing for it, but to go myself. Tarazona was about 10 kilometres away. I found the injured man in a state of collapse. I therefore gave him a further injection of morphine, put in seven to eight Michel's clips to hold the severed edges of the wound together, placed the arm in splints and, making him as comfortable as possible, took him by ambulance over the rough bumpy roads to the military hospital in Albacete. When the surgeon inspected the wound, he asked "Who put in these clips?" "I did" I replied. The surgeon nodded, "Quite good". Langer told me later that the injured German soldier had made good progress.

Quintanar de la Republica was a typical Spanish village whose grim stone farmhouses and barns were scattered amongst olive groves and fields of wheat, now bare with the approach of winter. On a high hill tall cypress trees looked over the walls of the cemetery, a landmark for the countryside.

Until 1936 (and now again with the restoration of the monarchy in Spain) the village had been Quintanar del Rey, but the former kings had never done much for it. The inhabitants had always been poor and illiterate. There was only one street and along this stood the barns which served as barracks for the Garibaldis. At one time two small factories had been producing olive oil but these were now closed. The largest of three churches, the one we had used as temporary barracks, had a tall, grey tower and stood on one side of the main square. On the other was the house now converted into the hospital.

Once a day the isolation of Quintanar was broken when a crowded bus left on the long winding journey to Albacete. Most able-bodied men had left, only the old men, women and children remained. The women rose at an unearthly hour to work in the fields. The children were ragged and went barefoot.

I arranged a regular clinic for the civilian population and had plenty of patients with various ailments or injuries. There were many cuts and soon I was a dab hand at suturing. The war had made food scarce. I could issue medicines, tonics and bandages, but sometimes, strictly against regulations, I slipped in tins of rationed condensed milk for a sick child. At first, the peasants regarded me with some suspicion, but after a while they took to me. I might even be invited to their home for a meal, and, once to my surprise, a chicken was produced from a secret hiding-place.

During the Civil War the Republic instigated improvements for the peasant population. In the schools the children, and adults too, were laboriously taught to read and write. Sanitary conditions were introduced. Poor people, they needed the help then. Now Spain enjoys the same material prosperity as other Western nations. The many English visitors to Spain today would be hard put to find evidence of the erstwhile extreme poverty.

With the coming of winter, the countryside became bleak and desolate and the rains made the roads even less passable. Already we experienced the occasional flurry of snow. The Garibaldi Battalion went on field manoeuvres. Just before Christmas we were stirred by news of a Republican offensive in the mountains near Teruel. The International Brigades, including the Garibaldis, would now be required at the front. As for me, a message had come to go immediately to Madrid to participate in a broadcast in which I would talk about my work and appeal to the British public to contribute food and medicaments for Spanish women and children.

On the outskirts of Madrid the car in which I was being driven came to a sudden halt. We had collided with a stationary lorry. Providentially, Miles Tomalin, an English writer, was just passing and gave me a lift to the radio station. I arrived in the nick of time. When it was my turn to speak, I was still a little out of breath. My appeal, as a consequence, sounded emotional and was judged very successful on that account.

I arrived back in Quintanar on Christmas eve with toys for the children which I had obtained, though with great difficulty. The Republican army had taken Teruel and so we celebrated with music and singing. The officers rendered sentimental Italian ballads and I contributed with "Annie Laurie".

Soon after the whole battalion assembled in the Square and, with the band playing and the troops singing the "Bandera Rossa", they marched off to the front. The gallant Garibaldis and I were parting and I would never see my friends again.

Chapter 10

A Divided Republic

At Quintanar a Spanish unit replaced the Italian Internationals. I put in a request that I be posted back as theatre nurse. Eventually, my successor arrived. He was a young Austrian and looked more like a student than a qualified doctor, but I was glad to hand over to him. Farewell, Quintanar de la Republica, for me you would now become only a memory.

I reported to Goryan and he asked me to go to England on a quick visit to obtain urgently required medical supplies. It was now early 1938. Hitler had taken over in Austria. For many people at home, the Spanish Republic was already defeated, but I remembered the courage of the young soldiers and the mountain ranges that Franco's troops would yet have to cross to reach Republican heartlands. So, when I spoke at meetings, I stressed the further resistance of our side.

I obtained instruments and drugs from John Bell and Croyden in Wigmore Street which were paid for by a sympathetic general practitioner, who had heard my appeal. I travelled back to Spain with Winifred Bates, Mary Slater and May MacFarlane whom I had not seen for sometime. Just as we were arriving at the English Flat in Barcelona, a car drew up and Langer stepped out. He looked grey and tired and seemed very relieved to see us. The war was going badly — land communication between Barcelona and Valencia was threatened. The whole Aragon front was crumbling. The International Brigades had been transferred to the northern sector and large numbers of casualties were being evacuated to new hospitals set up in the vicinity of Barcelona. Langer was very short of nurses as they had not yet arrived from the South. So May MacFarlane and I were immediately packed off in a lorry and driven to a large convent about an hour's journey from Barcelona which had been converted into a hospital. I proceeded to the ward

45

while May went to obtain some sleep in order to take over in the morning. Wounded were arriving as fast as during the battle on the Jarama. The improvised hospital already held about 200 dirty, bearded and worn-out men. I turned to one and asked, because of something familiar about him, "Are you English?" "Christ, woman!", he replied. "Don't give me shocks like that!" He had not expected any English nurses here. There were, in fact, many British amongst the casualties including George Fletcher, a Company Commander. They had passed through harrowing times, fighting, marching, then fighting again with men dropping out one after the other. In the end many had to swim the River Ebro under machine-gun fire to evade the Fascists. They asked after Wally Tapsell, Commissar of the British Battalion, who was missing, but I could not give them any information.

In the course of the next day, more International nurses arrived from the southern sector. Then came a message from Winifred Bates who had been in touch with Sybil Clarke in Valencia. Goryan was remaining in the South and had asked for me. There was no time to lose if I was to attempt the hazardous journey to the South. Back at the English Flat in Barcelona and picking up my equipment, I was in luck. The driver of a British ambulance, I believe it was Joe Coomes, was determined to cut through to the South to extricate British nurses, stranded in Uclés, near Madrid. With a spare Spanish driver we set out in the early morning. On the way to Tarragona we encountered aerial bombardment. Beyond Tarragona we came upon refugees — the sad spectacle that would be repeated again and again in Spain and then in many countries in World War II — pouring northwards on the coastal road in the opposite direction to ourselves, men, women and children on foot or on ox-carts piled high with bedding, furniture and other belongings. We reached Tortosa, now in ruins and deserted except for scattered groups of soldiers. The bridge over the Ebro was still standing and guarded and we were required to show our papers to drive across. A few kilometres further south we heard gun-fire. No civilians were now in sight, but then we came upon the first of our retreating forces. Small batches of soldiers with or without officers, even single men, who had lost their units in the long retreat, were tramping wearily northwards along the road. Suddenly we saw a few figures in khaki with red scarves around their necks — my friends, the Garibaldis! We stopped beside them "Salud!" I called. Blank, tired eyes stared up at me. Then two or three faces lit up in recognition "Salud Penny!" "Where is Roberto, the Commissar, where is Morelli, the Commandante?" I asked. They shook their heads, having lost contact with the battalion. I scribbled a quick note for Roberto in case they were reunited with their unit and then we drove on. Suddenly the road was empty. On the left was the blue Mediterranean, on the right were the mountains where we could see and hear exploding shells and where our troops were still fighting. Soon the Fascists would reach the sea at this spot and Republican Spain be cut in two.

As we drove on, we again encountered soldiers and refugees; we had reached the South, and soon arrived in Benicasim, a quiet seaside town where a base hospital for the International Brigades had once been sited. We drove through orange groves, passed Castellón and finally, late at night, we reached the English Villa in Valencia where I separated from Joe Coomes.

Sybil had Goryan's instructions for me. Soon I was heading north again in an ambulance, this time with Spanish personnel. At Sagunto our ambulance turned left off the coast road towards the province of Teruel. We climbed higher and higher into the mountains well past nightfall, when we stopped at a small house. We had reached our destination, for there was Goryan sitting by the light of an oil-lamp in earnest conversation with some officers.

His face lit up. "Salud Penny, I knew you would come". He looked gaunt, but was very pleased to receive the medical supplies from England. Also the food and cigarettes that I had brought with me.

The next morning I went to the new surgical unit. We were housed in two well-camouflaged barns amidst pine-trees high-up in the mountains. Now I was in an all-Spanish front line hospital attached to the Army of the Levant with the nearest Internationals hundreds of kilometres away. We had two operating-tables, but generally the equipment was sparse and I missed the surgical fitments provided in the special American vans when we were in Tarancón, Jarama and Brunete. However, the work of the Spanish surgeons and nurses was now quite outstanding and I had to admire the progress they had made in the past year.

We had been busy operating for three days when orders came to pack up and move at once. We were, in fact, retreating. We descended through the pine forest for several kilometres and set up our unit again in huts situated in a gorge which was now dry, but in winter probably held a raging torrent. So it went on, we had to retreat again and again. The young now totally Spanish army fought courageously, but was gradually forced towards Valencia and the sea. All the while, Fascist planes came over the mountains bombing and strafing the troops.

Part III

Back in England

Chapter 11

"You Were One of the Lucky Ones"

I have no recollection of what had happened when I became aware that I was on a stretcher, naked except for tight bandages round my chest and abdomen and that an orderly was attempting to give me an intra-muscular saline. It was the pain from this that had aroused me. Lifting my head a little, I saw red stains on the bandages round my chest; the left arm was also bandaged. With my right hand I felt what was congealed blood on my face, nostrils and ears. I tried to tell the young man that the fluid he was trying to pump into me was painful, but I could not think — no Spanish words came to mind. A doctor arrived who spoke English. I asked him where was I, because I seemed to be in a barn with many wounded people. He told me that the surgical unit had been bombed and that soon I would be evacuated down the line to a base hospital. Guessing my thoughts he said, "Yes, you were one of the lucky ones". He indicated that I had fractured ribs, abdominal wounds, an injured arm and numerous cuts and grazes. I was also coughing up blood, the result of contusion of the lungs.

Over the next few days we were taken down the mountains. I received morphine injections whilst lapsing in and out of semi-consciousness. Finally I found myself in a hospital in Benicasim, the only woman amongst the many wounded Spanish soldiers. Then we were on the move again; the Benicasim casualties were put on stretchers and taken by ambulance to the railway station and placed aboard railway trucks adapted to carry wounded. The train travelled slowly south. When we arrived at Castelión the air-raid sirens sounded. We were off-loaded and taken to a nearby shelter. The station and the train, with many wounded still on board, was hit by bombs; fire, death and destruction reigned everywhere. The rest of the journey by road on lorries to Valencia was a real nightmare.

D

In Valencia Military Hospital, I was put into an Officers' Ward. My overwhelming desire was to be taken to the English Villa. Several days passed during which I was given medicaments to relieve pain. I gathered I was ill, very ill and the surgeons wished to perform a laparotomy. No never, I protested, not here under wartime conditions. I had seen too many ill-consequences. As days went by I began to improve. It was sometime later that the English Authorities heard that there was a wounded English nurse in the Military Hospital. Arrangements were then made for me to be transferred and nursed at the English Villa where already two English nurses were looking after Sybil Clarke who was ill from food poisoning; they nursed both of us and I made further progress. The port area of Valencia had now become the target for bombing causing havoc all round us. The British Consul decided the villa should be evacuated. Sybil, accompanied by a nurse, was the first to go, being taken aboard a British merchant ship. Later, I was driven, along with other civilians, to the small port of Gandia south of Valencia. Here a British naval officer took us in a fast-moving launch to the cruiser HMS *Sussex*, waiting outside the three-mile-limit. Soon I was ensconced in a small spick and span cabin, far from the world I had just left; through the porthole I saw the Spanish coast receding. Surely I will be back in one month, two at the most, I was thinking. However, for me the Spanish Civil War had ended.

On the *Sussex* all was order and calm and I was able to obtain much required sleep and to enjoy a good cup of English tea. The naval medical officer had known Dr Sollenberger who was killed at Brunete; they had both been medical students at the London Hospital. The *Sussex* sailed to Marseilles where I was put on a plane and flown to Croydon Aerodrome. The Spanish Medical Aid Committee had arranged for an ambulance to take me to Hammersmith Hospital. Here everybody was the essence of kindness and I remember Dr Janet Vaughan looking after me. X-rays were taken and showed small fragments of shrapnel inside the abdomen. Again came talk of a laparotomy but, possibly because of my weak general condition, the doctors decided against it. Near Hammersmith Hospital was a Territorial Army firing range and Royal Air Force planes were flying low to and fro from Northolt Aerodrome. In my near-delirium I was back in Spain amongst the fighting of the Jarama and Brunete fronts or experiencing Fascist air raids on our positions in the mountains of Teruel Province. I was deteriorating and given oxygen. My family was sent for. In my lucid moments, however, I knew I must get better quickly in order to return to Spain, where I was urgently needed. What I really required, however, was peace and quiet. I was transferred to a private room in St. John's and Elizabeth Hospital, staffed by nuns. Through the window I saw green lawns, flowering shrubs and trees. Eventually I turned the corner and began to improve.

Because my skin was brown from the Spanish sun, the nuns assumed that I was a Spanish nurse from Franco's side. When they learnt the facts, they were dismayed but they listened, nevertheless, with sympathy when I related how Franco's German and Italian friends were bombing Spanish women and children day after day.

By mid-summer I was better and able to leave hospital. For convalescence I went to "Netherwood" in Hastings at the invitation of Vernon Symonds, a left-wing sympathiser, who ran a guest-house. When I first arrived I was thin as a rake, some six stone in weight, but I gathered strength rapidly, began to play tennis and joined in social activities. I met Mick and we fell in love; he was house surgeon at St. James's Hospital, Balham, and three months later we were married. Mick was the younger brother of T. R. (Tosko) Fyvel. He was at "Netherwood" with his family writing a book *"No Ease in Zion"*. Tosko had sympathised strongly with the struggle of Republican Spain against its Fascist opponents. He and his wife Mary encouraged our blossoming romance from the start. Furthermore, Mary helped me materially, for I had no money and practically no possessions with which to begin our married life. I must be forever grateful to Tosko and Mary for helping me to achieve what is now over fifty years of great love and happiness.

Mr William Gissane, an orthopaedic surgeon at the same hospital, later knighted for his work on accident prevention and construction of safer motor cars, was married on the same day. Mick's friend, Dr Gordon Osborne on the day of both weddings, got up with a colleague at an unearthly hour to go to Covent Garden to procure flowers for two bouquets. However, when Mick arrived at the Registry Office he was without my bouquet. The fact that he had been on duty during the night attending to ill patients made me forgive his forgetfulness.

This was early in December 1938. The International Brigades had been withdrawn from Spain. Sometime later I was walking along the Finchley Road in London, when a group of young men caught up with me and, as they passed by, they suddenly recognised and hailed me "Penny will you come with us to China?" They were ex-International Brigade medicals on their way to serve with the

Communist Forces. However, I had just rented a small flat in Belsize Road, Hampstead. Mick for sometime yet would continue to reside in the hospital to which he was attached and came home only when off duty. Going to China was not in my mind.

Many members of the International Brigades who had crossed into France were unable to return to their countries of origin because of their political colour. Those belonging to the Garibaldi Battalion were interned by the French authorities in camps where the inmates suffered great hardships. I received letters from Roberto, erstwhile commissar of the Garibaldis, during 1939 from one of these camps but later lost touch with him and I do not know of the ultimate fate of the interned Internationals when the Germans took over Petain's France.

Early in 1939, I decided to do private nursing and joined a London Nursing Agency who sent me on various assignments. I nursed a patient, a middle-aged Canadian lady, in a flat in Dolphin Square. She had a chest infection from which she made a good recovery only to lapse, much to the doctor's and my consternation, into a state of inebriation. We found a cache of whiskey and gin under her bed lodged between telephone directories and we thought our troubles were over. However, after her return to sobriety, came a further relapse of tipsiness. Eventually I discovered her ruse; she had struck a deal with the local off-licence to deliver gin and whiskey through the tradesmen's hatch. All's well that ends well. Cut off from her supply of drink my patient remained sober and subsequently she asked Mick's permission to take me on a motoring trip to the West Country. I was at first very reluctant to go, but she proved to be an excellent driver and we had a most enjoyable time. Moreover we stayed at first-class hotels which was a new experience for me. Eventually she returned home to Canada. Her name was Mrs Strange and jokingly I had coined the phrase "Strange by name and strange by nature".

On another occasion I was sent to a young couple, the Frosts, whose family owned a chain of grocery stores. Mrs Frost was indisposed but soon recovered. When I left they presented me with an Omega gold wrist-watch. During the war, I received from them an occasional parcel containing delicacies that had disappeared from the shops. The Omega watch was my companion for some thirty years or more. I used to take it for cleaning to a watch repairer in High Holborn, not far from St. Paul's Cathedral. His wife suffered from multiple sclerosis. When I telephoned after his retirement to Cornwall, I learnt that he had died shortly after the move from Central London and I felt great concern for his wife, left alone to cope with her disability. When later I took the watch to Harrods for repairs, they told me nothing more could be done for it, its infirmities being due to old age, which unfortunately, a doctor may have occasion to tell his patients.

Another time the nursing agency sent me to St. Thomas's Hospital, who required a nurse for night duty to "special" a seriously ill patient, Miss Banham, one time Matron-in-Chief to the London County Council, an ex-St. Thomas's nurse. She was in a coma suffering from cerebro-spinal meningitis and not responding to treatment. Miss Banham was a heavy woman, lifting and turning her was difficult, I gave her nasal feeds which pleased the houseman who was concerned over her nutrition. However, in spite of all efforts to save her, Miss Banham succumbed. There were also some indications that I was not physically fit for onerous nursing duties, but I did not heed these sufficiently.

By the end of March 1939, the Civil War in Spain ended in Franco's victory. Hitler invaded Czechoslovakia and threatened Poland. Russia and Germany signed a non-aggression treaty. World War II was about to begin.

Chapter 12

Onset of World War II

At the outbreak of war in September 1939, I became a night-sister at the Hampstead Air-Raid Precautions First-Aid Post. Immediate German air raids, resulting in heavy casualties, were expected. The London hospitals evacuated their patients to the Home Counties in order to free beds for expected air-raid victims. St. Mary's Hospital, to which my husband Mick was now attached, was converted into a type of casualty clearing station with surgical teams at the ready and extra operating-tables in place. The 'Emergency Medical Services', the EMS (not the one we hear so much about now, the European Monetary System) came into being. However, it was the period of the "phoney war" and Mick's main duty was to check the windows at St. Mary's to see that they had been properly blacked out. This proved to be a near-impossible task, the windows in the ramshackle building must have numbered hundreds, while some of them were inaccessible.

In the event, Hitler turned east against Poland which he crushed with his blitzkrieg. Our ARP station had no casualty work so we practised first aid on each other.

In the early summer of 1940, the Germans overran the Low Countries and France. The British Forces were evacuated from Dunkirk and in the clear skies of Southern England in the course of a beautiful summer the Royal Air Force and the Luftwaffe fought the Battle of Britain.

At the outbreak of war Mick had volunteered for the Royal Army Medical Corps and when his call-up papers arrived he went to Moss Bros. to obtain his uniform. Now it was a matter of making sure that his brass buttons were shiny and the Sam Browne belt polished. I thought he looked a fine, dashing officer, and, as a special treat, prepared a meal of fresh salmon with mayonnaise, new potatoes and a side plate of salad; but he was in such a hurry to catch the train and join the army to fight that he scarcely touched it. He need not have hurried for he was only off to Cookham, near Aldershot, where the RAMC had their depot. He was then sent to the Royal Engineers attached to 5th Corps Headquarters. A German invasion was imminent and secrecy was imposed. Road signs and the names of railway stations were removed. Mick's address was "British Home Forces, somewhere in England". I wanted to see him, but not knowing where he was stationed went to Waterloo Station where I had said good-bye when he departed for the army. I was, however, aware of his regimental flash, three silver galleons on a black and red background. I waited and, using my eyes, caught sight of some soldiers wearing the flash. I followed the soldiers and boarded the train with them. It was a journey into the unknown. When they alighted at their destination I did likewise. Establishing a friendly conversation I enquired about their Medical Officer, yes they knew him and would gladly deliver a note. Mick, in fact, was stationed in the Home Farm of Broadlands, the Mountbatten Estate on the banks of the River Test near Romsey. After receiving my note he arrived and we spent the night together at the Swan Inn, situated in the market place near the abbey. I returned to London, happy with our "brief encounter".

The Luftwaffe now turned to raiding London at night. The Blitz had begun. When the bombs fell on Hampstead, however, I was no longer at the ARP post, but a patient in the New End Hospital. My abdominal injuries received in Spain had flared up and an emergency operation was necessary. The ward was at the top of the building. Incendiary bombs fell and amidst the clatter of broken glass, fire, smoke and commotion, patients were taken to the basement. Over the next few days, my tummy became increasingly tight and uncomfortable. Suddenly I felt intense relief. The sutures had given way, the abdomen had burst open and I was taken hastily back to the operating-theatre for emergency repair. My condition deteriorated and it was decided to evacuate me to "Greenlands", the nursing home attached to the Royal Berkshire Hospital in Reading. No ambulance could be obtained and I was therefore taken to Reading in an adapted hearse. I was still alive, however, and a blood transfusion and M & B helped in my recovery. A medical board precluded me from being called-up for nursing. I therefore decided to embark on a new career.

Owing to the war effort, industry demanded a rapid increase in the labour force. Personnel Managers were required to oversee the recruitment of this labour intake, largely composed of women, to introduce them to industrial processes and to attend to their welfare both at and off their place of work. I applied for this type of post and was selected by the Ministry of Labour for a course in Personnel Management at Edinburgh University. So with the restrictions on the presence of wives now less stringent, I decided to visit Mick who was stationed in Minstead a small village in the New Forest, until the term began in Edinburgh.

I remember a long, exhausting walk from Lyndhurst station carrying a suitcase. After reaching the town of Lyndhurst, I turned right in the direction of Cadnam roundabout, walked past the kennels of the foxhounds and then took a minor road on the left to arrive at Minstead and found accommodation in a little house off the village green across a cattle-grid (which also keeps out the forest ponies). I was thus able to see my husband when he was off duty.

The British Army, which had been successfully evacuated from Dunkirk, was now scattered over the English countryside and had to rearm and retrain to fight possibly in Britain, but actually in the Far East and Burma, North Africa, Sicily, Italy and finally, North West Europe. Most soldiers came from towns and cities and the country was something new to them. Many found inaction and waiting about rather tedious, but most places had friendly country pubs such as "The Trusty Servant" in Minstead, where time could be passed in a pleasant manner.

The young local VADs had little to do; Mick, therefore, decided to utilise the gardener's bothy at Minstead Lodge as a sick-bay for minor ailments amongst the troops, thus enabling the VADs to look after them. During the bombing of Southampton a young soldier who was with the troops fighting the fires became ill and collapsed. He was brought to the sick-bay in Minstead on an open lorry. When Mick examined him he diagnosed pneumonia. He thereupon sent me a message that I should come and help the VADs with the nursing of the ill soldier: just at that time General Bernard Montgomery, then commander of the 5th Corps, was inspecting the troops on the village green. I remember this occasion very well, because it was raining cats and dogs and the troops were drenched to the skin. At the end of the parade the Colonel took Monty to the sick-bay in the bothy of the Lodge. When Monty came to the very ill soldier, he was very displeased. Why had the man not been transferred to the military hospital at Netley on the other side of Southampton water in accordance with the regulations? Mick replied, that the soldier had been too ill to stand the journey to Netley. Monty seemed reasonably mollified by the explanation. The young soldier subsequently made a good recovery.

Minstead, situated in a beautiful corner of the New Forest, was peaceful enough and my spirits and health improved rapidly but, at night, we heard the drone of the Heinkels on the way to bomb the provincial cities and when Southampton was raided fires could be seen raging in the distance. Suddenly the home front was to have a breather; it was June 1941 and Hitler invaded Russia. I was now on my way to Edinburgh University for my studies.

In Edinburgh I had no difficulty in finding a flat in one of the large grey stone buildings which I shared with other students. In spite of the war, life for the student body was relatively relaxed. I remember pleasant gatherings attended also by members of the University staff. I felt that as a 'mature student' I enjoyed a certain standing.

The members of the Ministry's Training Course were attached to the faculty of social science. This was of high calibre. I did not experience the 'cultural shock' as when starting out at Hillcroft College in spite of the passage of eight eventful years. The contents of the course comprised, but in greater detail, the "machinery of government" lectures at Hillcroft. All enactments and regulations covering work, health, sickness and safety as they had evolved from the nineteenth century onwards were included. We were expected to be fully conversant with them at the end of the course.

After a period of study at Edinburgh I was sent to Halex Ltd. in Essex, a large factory making plastic goods for civilians and the armed forces. I gained very good practical experience under supervision by their Personnel Department. I became a member of the Institute of Personnel Management. Soon I obtained a post with Messrs J. Lyons as Personnel Manager at their Greenford factory which was a very busy plant processing and packaging food for the forces and civilian population. It was a well-planned and well-run organisation, much superior to the noisy and dirty factories as I remembered them from my Tottenham days.

The employees' work was not particularly difficult or stressful and, considering the wartime circumstances, the atmosphere was quite cheerful. I had to introduce green labour, mostly women, to their working environment and dealt with welfare, accommodation problems, money matters and the emotional difficulties arising through separation from menfolk and members of their families. I attended meetings of the management and brought up the main concerns of the workforce. Lyons was still largely a family business and what struck me particularly was the detailed knowledge possessed by the management of their extensive factory and its many employees. As companies grow, turn into conglomerates and multi-nationals, much in areas of personal and public relations must be lost. What do people know or feel today about Allied Lyons? Where are the Nippies, Teashops and Corner Houses?

After a time at my job with Lyons, I had a short holiday and visited my husband now attached to a general military hospital in Bangor, County Down in Northern Ireland; a pleasant seaside town. I also managed a quick trip to Dublin, staying at the Shelbourne Hotel, enjoying the bright lights and the shops full of goods which could be bought without coupons. While in Bangor, Mick suggested that I leave Messrs J. Lyons in order to study medicine. He felt I might become a surgeon. It would be necessary, however, to start at the very beginning of the medical course and to take the science subjects of zoology, botany, physics and chemistry, required for the first MB examinations. I obtained a place for the preclinical course at Birmingham University and secured accommodation with Hillcroft College which had been evacuated from Surbiton to Bourneville at the outbreak of the war. Meanwhile Mick had been posted overseas.

Soon I was dissecting the dogfish, looking down the microscope at botanical specimens or performing experiments in physics. At the time regular air mail letter cards were arriving from Iraq, where Mick was now stationed, giving instructions in my subjects — a sort of improvised correspondence course — as well as an account of his activities.

Chapter 13

A Passage to India, Persia and Iraq

I now tell the stories unfolded in Mick's letters at the time of his journey to Persia and Iraq. They seem to be relevant to recent events. In 1942 he sailed from Birkenhead in a large convoy aboard HMS *Abosso* of the Elder Dempster line which had been converted into a troop-ship. The convoy could only proceed according to the speed of the slowest vessel, the ships and their escorting destroyers zigzagging to avoid German U-boats. The flotilla of ships, extending to the horizon, was an impressive sight. On one occasion the convoy was brought to a halt while someone who had died was buried at sea. Immediately the rumour spread that U-boats had infiltrated the motionless ships and were about to unleash their torpedoes. However, the moment of danger passed, no U-boats had struck and the convoy was on its way.

It stopped off the coast of West Africa at Freetown where provisions and fuel were taken on board. The ships were kept well out to sea supposedly beyond the flying range of malaria-bearing mosquitos from the mainland or so the medical officers were told. However, when the journey was resumed, cases of malignant malaria began to occur amongst officers and men. Probably the wind had carried the mosquitos to the ships. Malaria is still the most widespread tropical disease. Those off on long-haul holidays are well advised to take most serious measures to avoid catching malaria, which, especially in its malignant form, remains a most unpleasant illness.

The convoy reached the Cape of Good Hope. Some ships, including the *Abosso*, docked at Cape Town; others proceeded to Durban. The men were granted shore leave, and received with extraordinary warmth and hospitality by the local people. Fresh citrus fruit totally unobtainable at home was abundant. Very pleasant memories of their South African break during the long journey to the Middle East and India must still be retained by many ex-servicemen alive today.

I have a friend, a colleague from Hillcroft College days, who now lives in Cape Town. I would have liked to have visited her. However, my flying days are over and there do not seem to be any boats now sailing to South Africa. What has happened to the famous Union Castle Line and all its wonderful ships? Gone, forever!

The *Abosso* continued her journey three days later. She was bound for Bombay. The convoy was very much smaller. Most ships had departed for Suez taking reinforcements to the armies in the Western Desert. Suddenly, an outbreak of diarrhoea and vomiting affecting many of those aboard the *Abosso*. However, recovery was rapid. Recently, the liner *Canberra* during its Mediterranean cruises experienced rather similar explosive epidemics without their precise cause being established. Possibly a virus that thrives on crowded ships is to blame.

The *Abosso* docked in Bombay and the troops disembarked and spent one night ashore. On the following day they re-embarked on another troop-ship bound for the Persian Gulf. (The story has it that on a later voyage the *Abosso* was cut in two, with heavy loss of life, by the liner *Queen Mary*, zigzagging at speed). Mick's brief glimpse of Bombay and India had impressed upon him the great multitude of its people. It was now the middle of August and, as the ship entered the Gulf, the intense heat and humidity struck the unacclimatised troops. Some had not even been issued with tropical kit and were still wearing khaki. The unending, profuse sweating induced by the great humidity resulted in almost everyone suffering from prickly heat. Then cases of heat-stroke and heat exhaustion cropped up. Mick and his colleagues improvised a heat-stroke centre in the hold of the ship with blocks of ice obtained from the cooks in the galley and were able to treat the patients with some degree of success. The ship arrived at Basra in Iraq (where some of the heavy fighting of the recent Iran-Iraq War took place). The troops were to be disembarked during the relatively cool of the night before the searing heat of the rising sun would have to be faced. In fact, dawn was already breaking when the troops were finally off the ship and marching to their destination, an encampment in the adjoining desert of Shaiba. Mick observed a trail of water to the rear of the column of soldiers. What in heaven's name was happening? The troops had been provided with Indian Army-type fabric water-bottles, but these had not been properly soaked prior to issue which caused them to leak until they were empty. When the soldiers reached their destination, now under the blazing sun, they had no water to quench their thirst and to replenish their fluid loss. Moreover, they had to erect large tents for sleeping quarters. The situation was calamitous! One by one soldiers were dropping prostrated by heat-stroke. Thankfully an ambulance arrived and the casualties were taken to a heat-stroke centre. Not all survived. British troops had served in Iraq during World War I. The lessons of the deleterious effects of intense heat should have been borne in mind. Mick was very sad to lose some of his men on the very day of their arrival in Iraq. He felt the troops had not been given a chance to become properly acclimatised before exposure to the extreme conditions of the Persian Gulf and Iraq desert. Nor had the arrangements for disembarkation been good.

Soon Mick's unit (3rd Corps Signals) was on its way from Basra to Baghdad by road and again became dogged by misfortune. A fierce sandstorm erupted. The road, often no more than a track, was obliterated. Lorries carrying the soldiers lost their way, others sank into the soft sand and had to be winched out. Further heat-stroke casualties resulted. The romance of passing Biblical towns like Babylon and Ur of the Chaldees was diminished by these misfortunes. The unit moved on into Persia and encamped in a mountainous area near the oil-town of Kermanshah. Tents were put up on a barren, rocky slope and dug in against the cold of the approaching winter. Lush meadows in the valley below were out of bounds because they swarmed with malarious mosquitos.

British troops had been assembled in a hurry near Kermanshah to meet a possible German advance through the Caucasian mountains towards the Middle East. So it was that Mick by chance came across Reuben, one of my young twin brothers and took him out for what Reuben called a schoolboy's treat. He was serving with the Wiltshires in the 4th Indian Division.

The German threat, however, was stemmed by the Russians. The 4th Indian Division and other commands moved to the Western Desert to take part in the Battle of El Alamein, and later in Italy in the fierce battles for the monastery at Monte Cassino. Here Reuben was killed and later my brother George came across his grave in the Minturno Cemetery.

Mick's unit, still in Persia, but having moved from Kermanshah, was encamped for the winter on a plain near the Holy City of Quom. The golden domes of the mosques could be seen from the campsite, but the town was strictly out of bounds. Allegedly the mullahs were fanatics and anti-British. Possibly the late Ayatollah Khomeini was earning his spurs preaching anti-Western sentiments. The English camp was situated beside a single-track railway line and, all day long, trains passed carrying war materials from the

Gulf ports to Tehran destined for the Russians. Our other supply route to the Russians was by perilous convoys round the North Cape, to Murmansk. Some forty years later I was to cruise in these waters on board the *'Sea Princess'*.

Mick became very busy owing to an outbreak of diphtheria amongst the troops affecting not only the throat but also the skin. Many soldiers were suffering from 'desert sores' and these became infected with diphtheria bacilli.

In one of his letters Mick related that, though the soldiers had received lectures on prevention of venereal disease, they nevertheless caught infections in the brothels of Tehran, even though these were out of bounds. He recalls a sapper who had refused vaccination against smallpox allegedly on conscientious grounds. While on leave the sapper visited a brothel; this landed him not only with venereal disease, but also with a severe attack of smallpox from which he all but died.

The recent elimination of smallpox through the work of the World Health Organisation marks an outstanding achievement of preventative medicine.

Whilst I was doing fever training, epidemics of smallpox were still breaking out from time to time. Patients were not routinely admitted to the Eastern Fever Hospital, however, instead they were sent to Joyce Green Hospital. Previously patients were treated in a special hospital ship moored on the Thames Estuary, where strict isolation could be assured.

Mick was posted to 29 British General Hospital in Tehran. This was originally a splendid civilian hospital completed just before the war under supervision by German architects. Tehran was beautifully situated with snow-capped mountains on its northern aspect. However, open sewers flowed by the side of the broad boulevards. The rich had fine houses, but many of the poor lived in hovels. In the bazaars and in the shops goods and food were in plentiful supply. The civilians appeared aloof, enmeshed in their religion and poverty. Few women were to be seen on the streets.

The Russians from the north and the British from the south had occupied Persia earlier in the war and formed a common frontier in Tehran. At that time a stream of lorries filled with Polish men, women and children was arriving. They had been transported from camps in Siberia and the arctic region over a thousand miles away.

Not long after the outbreak of war the Russians had marched into Eastern Poland in accordance with the provision of the Ribbentrop—Molotov pact. They rounded up large numbers of Poles, especially those of the upper crusts, and took them away to labour camps. Many Polish officers were shot by the Russians and buried in mass graves in the forest of Katyn, as the Russians have recently admitted, having previously blamed the Nazis for this massacre. After the Germans invaded Russia and the Russians became our allies, they agreed to release their Polish prisoners and allowed them to travel to Persia. They reached Tehran emaciated and exhausted from their ordeals. Some, unfortunately, gorged themselves on the lavish foodstuffs they found in the shops, which made them ill, and a few even died. However, most embarked on the process of physical and mental rehabilitation and revived their culture with song, dance and renewed adherence to the Roman Catholic religion. The men of military age joined the forces of General Anders. At the grim battles for the Monte Cassino Monastery, the Poles fought valiantly and sustained heavy casualties (the Polish losses at Monte Cassino are commemorated in ceremonies to this day). The released Polish civilians, eventually settled in Britain, mostly in Scotland and have integrated into British society. Few were willing to return to Poland whilst it remained a communist regime, but now Poland is changing, some of the Poles living in Britain may elect to go back. Pro-Russian sentiment was strong amongst the British forces in Persia, for the Russians at that time were putting up the main resistance to the Germans, later in the year to culminate in the battle of Stalingrad when a whole German army was surrounded by the Russians and forced to surrender.

When Mick looked after Polish patients admitted to the 29 General Hospital, he found it difficult to listen without considerable emotion to their stories of hardship and torment, wantonly inflicted on them by the Russians. Yet pointers to the future Russian stance towards their Western allies already existed. Although the British were bringing vast quantities of supplies from the Gulf and handing them over to the Russians, the latter allowed no fraternisation or contacts between the troops. It was a curious relationship between allies, heralding the later Iron Curtain and the Cold War.

In 1943, a meeting took place in Tehran between Churchill, Roosevelt and Stalin. By this time Mick had been posted to 25 Combined General Hospital in the Shaiba desert. This was a unit of the Indian Army and the Indian officers were not averse to expressing their great impatience to be rid of the British Raj. However, as Mick wrote, the Indian chefs managed to produce, amidst the dirt and dust of the desert, some very appetising, tasty and much appreciated meals.

Chapter 14

Victory in Europe and Japan

Meanwhile what happened to me was as follows: Miss Ashby, whom I have already mentioned when she became Principal of Hillcroft College during my attendance as a student there nine years ago, had retired but when, at the outbreak of the war, the college was evacuated to Bourneville, she was recalled to act again as principal. Sometime later she suddenly became very ill with pneumonia. No nurse could be found for her, owing to their call-up. So I took on the job of nursing her, day and night through the crisis to recovery. Unfortunately the strain on me was severe; my old troubles, due to war injury, were rekindled and I was admitted into Queen Elizabeth Hospital, Birmingham and operated on by Professor Gemmel of Birmingham University. The Army recalled Mick from Iraq, on compassionate grounds. By the time he arrived in England I was still ill but gradually improving. During my convalescence Mick told me how he travelled from Baghdad to Damascus across the desert in the Nairn coach, a long and tedious journey; then by train to the British base at Ismaila in the Canal Zone. An army surgeon, who had purloined a case of captured German surgical instruments in the Western Desert, on learning that Mick was on his way home, asked him to take the case to the United Kingdom and forward it to his home address. Foolishly, Mick agreed. While on the train to Alexandria, realising his own kit was difficult enough to transport, he opened the window of the compartment and ejected the instrument case, hoping someone would find and make some money from it. In Alexandria, Mick joined the first convoy to sail unmolested through the Mediterranean, the result of the Allies having cleared the Germans and Italians from North Africa.

When I had fully recovered, I had to face the fact that much time had been lost in pursuit of my medical studies, so, even though I had made good progress, I gave them up.

An advertisement in the *Journal of Personnel Management* led to my joining the staff of the Aftercare Association for Physically Handicapped Youth, a charitable organisation setting out to find suitable employment for disabled youngsters after they left school. It had a central office in Westminster where Miss Winder, a capable and experienced social worker, was in charge. She supervised me and my fellow field-workers. First we made contact with the young people, if they were still at school and many were at special schools for the physically handicapped (such as one I remember at Brooke Green in Hammersmith). They were interviewed along with their parents and teachers. If, however, they had already left school and were at home, it was then necessary to visit them. I well recall making tedious journeys by public transport, tramping along dingy streets, heavily scarred by bomb damage, climbing many flights of dark tenement stairs, as there were no functioning lifts, and having knocked several times on the door of the flat, receiving no reply. The parents were usually out at work and the youth perhaps had been instructed not to open the door to callers. I remember one occasion when I had such an unrewarding call which I had repeated after a lapse of about one hour, Miss Winder receiving a call from the mother complaining that I had not visited, although she said that her son was in. It turned out that the boy was stone-deaf and all my thumping on the door had been in vain. It was a welcome change to find a parent at home and the youngster available for interview.

Armed with school and medical reports I would form an opinion as to the youth's potential capabilities for work. I would then visit factories and workshops and discuss possible placement of my charges with the manager, personnel officer or foreman. Sometimes I appealed to their patriotism or even compassion to persuade them to employ my youngsters. Reports of my endeavours were given to Miss Winder. We carefully and in detail discussed the demands of the job in relation to the physical disabilities of my charges. The reports and our conclusions were filed and brought out when follow-up visits were made.

After a time I knew a great deal about the type of work going on in London's factories and workshops, particularly in the Hammersmith area which was my special patch. I came to be in a good position to match my handicapped youths with available jobs. I was seeking to place them in the open market and not in sheltered workshops specially adapted for the handicapped. So there were many difficulties and, perhaps not unexpectedly, the

E

fall-out rate was high. Matters were not helped by the coming of flying bombs and rockets which added further distress to London's inhabitants. My home, a bungalow in South London, which I had been fortunate in finding when I became a social worker, twice suffered damage from flying bombs, though thankfully not from a direct hit. 'Wimpey' men, mainly Irish, employed on bomb damage repair were billeted on me for some time, so all in all I kept quite busy.

Mick was now posted to Stoke-on-Trent, where he enjoyed the lovely countryside, so near the town and ideal for walking. The potteries seemed very ancient, using methods and kilns dating back to the eighteenth century. However, he remembers visiting one modern, all-electric works, probably Wedgewood's. He was subsequently moved to Lincoln and found visits to the cathedral, castle and the old district very interesting. It was at Lincoln, during a home leave from the Spanish Civil War, that I had one of my most successful meetings to raise funds on behalf of Spanish Medical Aid.

Mick's unit, 115 General Hospital, then moved to Scarborough awaiting its turn to cross the Channel and join the British Liberating Armies (BLA) in North West Europe. Also waiting near Scarborough were the men of the 1st Airborne Division. I briefly visited Mick and met several officers who had been colleagues at St. Mary's. The men were at the peak of their training, raring to go and play their part which was to be in the future Battle of Arnhem. Brigadier R. E. Urquart, their commander, portrayed by Sean Connery in the film 'A Bridge Too Far', died recently.

Having crossed the Channel, 115 General Hospital opened up in what had been a convalescent home for children at Den Haan, near Ostend, just in time to receive many casualties, both British and German, from fierce fighting round the island of Walcheren. Here the Germans held key positions denying ships access to the Scheldt Estuary and the port of Antwerp. They had to be dislodged. Until Antwerp was opened, the British Army had only the very long supply line from the Normandy beach-heads. The 'Battle of the Bulge', when the Germans nearly broke through the Ardennes, was a reminder they were far from finished.

The Dutch had to endure another winter of occupation and near starvation until, in the following year, the British armies crossed the Rhine and took the war into the heart of Germany. The death camp of Belsen was liberated and the people at home saw the terrible scenes depicted on the cinema screen. Until then, the full extent of the Nazi horror had not been realised.

General Porritt, advisor in surgery to the BLA, visited 115 General Hospital and gave his impressions of Belsen. Arthur Porritt, was a surgeon at St. Mary's Hospital when Mick had been a student. He became President of the Royal College of Surgeons and Governor-General of New Zealand. What a distinguished career! His son Jonathon, formerly director, Friends of the Earth, is now often in the limelight.

At last it was VE Day and then, following the Hiroshima and Nagasaki atomic bombs, VJ Day. After learning about genocide of the Jews, we heard of atrocities in prisoner of war camps, of starvation, disease and death suffered by allied soldiers at the hands of the Japanese.

Mick was now in Hanover, which had been badly bombed and was in ruins. The Germans were facing a grim winter, but had begun the job of rehabilitating their country and resumed performances in the opera house, which were much enjoyed by British military personnel.

Mick was demobilised early in 1946. He looked less smart in his 'demob' suit than in his uniform, but now we would be together. He was going to specialise in dermatology. I continued my work with the Aftercare Association. Grim conditions persisted with no let-up in rationing and a severe winter in 1947 brought icy roads and a fuel crisis. Plans were afoot for Health and Social Services to be organised on a national basis. A new type of social worker, the Disablement Resettlement Officer, the DRO, would be created who would have the task of placing the physically handicapped, both adult and juvenile, in suitable employment. The work of the Aftercare Association was destined to be absorbed into that of such statutory officers. The suggestion was made that I should become a DRO. However, instead of dealing with the sympathetic and efficient Miss Winder, I foresaw a host of bureaucratic rules and regulations, so I backed away and decided to remain at home.

Chapter 15

A Bungalow in Streatham Hill

The early nineteen fifties were hardly outstanding years for Britain. After-effects of the war were lifting very slowly and only a few signs such as the Festival of Britain in 1951 showed that the country was springing into life again. In many London bomb-sites, wild flowers were growing in profusion bringing an unexpected splash of colour to the scene. It was the time of "angry young men" and plays of the "kitchen sink" variety. For me it was to be a period of domesticity accompanied by other activities and pastimes which led to unexpected joys. Later I resumed new responsibilities, as I shall relate.

The bungalow I found in the later stages of the war was attractively situated in Streatham Hill overlooking at the rear an open space with allotments and two tennis-courts, and enjoying extensive views stretching over South London towards the Crystal Palace. I turned to decorating the bungalow, becoming a dab hand at rubbing down, painting and paper hanging. As far as I recall the phrase 'do it yourself' had not then come into usage.

I cultivated the garden and after a time it became a spectacle of colour and a focus of attraction for the neighbourhood. One morning a whole row of floribunda roses had been uprooted and the bushes were gone. The vandals had come to Streatham Hill.

I made good friends amongst the neighbours. We had been thrown together at the time of the flying bombs. One of the flight paths of these disagreeable 'doodle-bugs', with their throbbing engines and comet-like tail of flame, frequently lay right overhead. Several cut out and fell close by causing extensive damage and injury. Like me, after the war, most women were staying at home for the drive to go out to work had not really begun. We and the neighbours were nearly all living in rented houses or maisonettes;

the landlords, Leigham Court Estate, were charging reasonable rent. So the husbands' salaries sufficed to sustain the families' living standards. We were a sociable group, regularly dropping in on one another for chin-wags over cups of tea or coffee and playing the occasional game of tennis.

Soon after return to civilian life Mick, being a doctor, was able to purchase a car. This was a Wolseley 8, apparently a favourite of Lord Nuffield himself. Perhaps possessing a chassis and a substantial steel body, it was somewhat underpowered but the Wolseley served us well for over ten years. I learnt to drive and so was able, when Mick did not need the car, to take relatives and friends on trips to the coast and countryside.

Mick and I had been on a camping holiday in the first summer of our marriage, not long before the outbreak of the war. We borrowed a small tent, bought a Primus stove, a few cooking utensils and camped out in the grounds of "Netherwood" in Hastings, where we first met. A lesson of camping, not to pitch a tent under trees because of the drip-drip of rain, was soon learnt. The open-air life had whetted my appetite for more. So after the war, we regularly set out with tent and car on camping holidays at home and abroad; roads were still relatively uncluttered and it was a wonderful way to savour the delights of the countryside.

In the first summer after the war we camped on a small farm near Dartmoor. The farm only had a few cows. When it was milking time, Mr Colton, the farmer, called each by name and they came trotting to the shed. Mr Colton chatted to his cows while milking and I believe this increased their yield. We saw Dartmoor in its changing moods, travelled along narrow Devonshire lanes to old villages and towns, admired the beauty of the estuaries and listened to the song of the skylarks or the cry of the sea-birds — all this being in marked contrast to London's greyness and austerity at that time. We bathed off Bigbury Sands and, at low tide; crossed over to Burgh Island.

The next summer saw us in Normandy. British cars on the continent were still uncommon and passing GBs greeted each other by tooting their horns. The first night we pitched the tent near Honfleur by the side of a ruined bunker of the Atlantic Wall — a place with a spooky atmosphere. We searched in the war cemeteries for the grave of Harry, my young brother, for he had been killed not long after the Normandy landings, but learnt from the War Graves Commission in Bayeux that he had no grave, his body never having been found. Poor Harry, he had only been married three months before he was killed; he was barely twenty-one years old. His twin brother Reuben, killed in Italy, had been unmarried.

The French were very active in rebuilding their devastated country. They were hard at work before seven o'clock in the morning. Bananas and oranges, still unheard of at home, were available in the French markets. We brought home a large tin of ham and opened it at a party. The eyes of our friends lit up, everybody was becoming a little tired of spam. On a subsequent visit to France we toured the Châteaux of the Loire and camped within the grounds of Chenonceaux Castle, a really impressive location. A few days later having pitched the tent on the banks of the Loire we were awakened well before dawn by sounds of approaching men. These emanated from a group of fishermen, 'early birds' who had already 'caught their worms' and were about to use them as bait.

Some years later, again touring France, we erected the tent at the edge of a field. In the early morning, we heard muffled voices — with some apprehension, as it was the year of the murder of Sir Jack Drummond and his family in Southern France. The voices, however, receded and, later emerging from the tent, we found an enormous mushroom on the bonnet of our dusty car and scrawled in the dust was the caption *"Je suis bon"*.

In Switzerland, while seeking out a listed campsite, we travelled up and up into the mountains. The metalled road gave way to a mere track. All signs of civilisation had long been left behind. A patch of green was finally reached. Forbidding pine forests were nearby. "This is it" said Mick, getting out of the car. "Look at the map." He put up the tent. I cooked a meal and prepared for bed. "No need to be afraid of wolves. They do not attack humans", Mick said teasingly. But I knew otherwise, had I not seen voracious wolves depicted on television? That night, if wolves did not howl, the elements certainly were very noisy. We got up in the morning to a big surprise. All round was covered in snow, a beautiful sight. I bathed in a gushing ice-cold waterfall close by, which was most exhilarating!

Mick and I particularly enjoyed our stay on the Isle of Skye. The campsite was not far from Portree. It was towards the latter half of May and the days were very long. On motoring past a glade full of bluebells we suddenly found ourselves enmeshed in the middle of a motorcade with cars to the front and cars to the back of us — and no chance of breaking away as the road was so narrow. The procession of cars including ours was heading for Dunvegan Castle and soon entered the grounds. It was the special occasion of the gathering of MacLeods from all over the world at the home of the chief of their clan and they were about to celebrate. Seemingly, for the day, we too had become MacLeods. After listening to speeches, enjoying entertainments, partaking of lavish refreshments, we were taken for a trip in a launch to view the majestic medieval castle from the sea and to look at seals basking in the sun. A very memorable day for two involuntary gatecrashers.

When walking along Palace Road in Streatham Hill, I passed a barrow boy. He was holding a tiny puppy and I saw a pair of appealing eyes looking at me. "How much?" I asked. "Five bob" came the reply. I gave the boy the money and carried the puppy home. I called him Peter, but it was a female and so became Peta. Peta was a mongrel with a lot of whippet in her, as she grew into maturity she became a great runner. We had exhilarating romps and many happy times together on Streatham Common where she exhibited her prowess. Sometimes I would take Peta with me into town. One day Mick showed me a paragraph in the Londoner's Diary of the *Evening Standard*. It told of how, on the previous hot day, a lady was seen walking along Regent Street with her dog. Suddenly the lady stopped and produced a thermos flask and a saucer from her bag. She placed the saucer on the pavement, poured water from the flask into it and gave her dog a drink while passers-by looked on in amusement. "That sounds like you and Peta," Mick said. He was right.

The story of Peta ends sadly; she became ill with a growth and had to be put to sleep. My emotional reaction was deep; I decided against having another dog.

One day a tall mast, very much like a telegraph pole, with horizontal struts, appeared on the roof of a neighbour's house. It was an aerial — television had arrived. In due course we obtained a television set, and though the black and white image was small, we and a few invited neighbours much enjoyed the spectacle of the coronation of Elizabeth II. This was in 1953. Winston Churchill retired and Anthony Eden became Prime Minister. Suddenly, in 1956, the Suez crisis broke. Then, under Harold MacMillan, many new homes were built, but alas, also vast housing estates consisting of tenements and tower blocks. Popularity of the temporary 'prefabs' should have indicated the type of accommodation which would accord with the wishes of most people.

Part IV

Happenings in London

Chapter 16

The Road to Harley Street

One of my husband's post-war appointments was as consultant dermatologist to St. James's Hospital in Balham. (He had been a junior doctor there when I married him). His predecessor was Dr O'Donovan of the London Hospital, who went to St. James's once a week to advise on the many patients with skin disorders. He travelled from Central London by tube to Balham Underground Station and then took a taxi for the relatively short distance to St. James's Hospital. The taxi was kept waiting while Dr O'Donovan saw all the skin patients at a rapid rate. The task completed, he returned in the waiting taxi to Balham Station and was soon back in his consulting rooms in Harley Street. Dr O'Donovan was a formidable personality about whom many anecdotes were told. One concerns the occasion when he was on the hustings as a prospective Member of Parliament and a heckler called out "You are only the pox-doctor from the Whitechapel Road". Dr O'Donovan stopped in his tracks, bowed in the direction of his interlocutor and exclaimed "And who should know better than you my friend!"

Mr Norman Tanner, a surgeon at St. James's, achieved such a reputation that visitors from all over the world came to watch him operate. However, additional presence of spectators in the small theatre created a bit of a jam. An American was heard to remark "What great surgery, but why do they make him operate in a dog kennel?"

The National Health Service, instituted in 1948 had the difficult task of rebuilding and refurbishing our antiquated hospitals. St. James's was one of the first to obtain a new out-patients department and operating suites. So Mr Tanner was promoted from his dog kennel. During the initial dermatological clinic held in the brand-new spick and span out-patients, a large bottle of the dye gentian violet was spilt all over the floor producing an indelible stain. What a christening! No apologies could soothe Sister's outraged feelings.

A new out-patient department was also built at North Middlesex Hospital, Edmonton, a predominantly working-class area. Adjacent to the new block was a very large car-park. When Mick looked out of the clinic window, at first he saw no cars, but soon there were a few, then more and more, until a veritable sea of cars obstructed his view. What had happened? How could this have come about? Harold MacMillian knew; had he not said "You have never had it so good."?

The Royal Earlswood Hospital for the mentally subnormal was in the news recently because of a connection with Royalty. I had worked there for a while before the National Health Service was introduced. It was then markedly overcrowded and extremely shabby. A report in a medical journal stated "Considerable financial expenditure has enabled the hospital to be refurbished to modern standards and the pleasant gardens and swimming-pool add to the amenities"; so this is good progress.

Dr Ronald MacKeith was appointed consultant paediatrician to Guy's Hospital not long after being demobilised from the Royal Navy. I had met him before the war when he was resident physician in charge of the children's ward at St. James's Hospital and became very friendly with him. The main disease of infants and young children at that time was diarrhoea and vomiting. Infants with 'D and V' rapidly became dehydrated and many required intravenous saline. After an evening off-duty, Ronnie might return to find that several babies had been admitted. He would then have to embark on the onerous task of cutting down on the tiny veins of his little patients to insert a needle for the saline infusions, a labour that might take him into the early hours of the morning.

One of the great advances since those days is the advent of 'disposables', sharp needles, syringes and tubing and so on, discarded after use, which are part and parcel of modern therapeutic regimens.

Ronnie MacKeith was part of a group of paediatricians who brought about a revolution in hospital paediatric practice making it much more humane. Children's wards are now happy places where the presence of parents is encouraged. Parents may even sleep on hospital premises. Nurses pick up and cuddle their charges. Noise and boisterousness are allowed. Play therapy is used to help recovery. Cheerful pictures and posters hang on the walls of the wards. I seem to recall that at Guy's, the Department of Medical

Illustration was used to plan the decoration of the children's wards.

Ronnie was interested in developmental aspects of paediatrics. He was very active in the Spastics Society and in other organisations concerned with neurological defect in children. He was also a bit of an eccentric. One of his parlour tricks at parties apparently consisted of eating daffodil blooms (though when he used to visit me, early in the war he preferred a good meal!) I remember an occasion when Ronnie took me to a cinema in the West End to see Greta Garbo, after which, in the Haymarket, he kept on embracing me loudly exclaiming "Ninotchka, Ninotchka, I love you", to my intense embarrassment as passers-by stopped and stared. Ronnie's memory is much revered.

My husband's main hospital, St. Mary's, was situated in Paddington, north of the River Thames and he was experiencing traffic hold-ups, especially when crossing the river. I, therefore, began to look for a flat in the Maida Vale, St. John's Wood and Marylebone areas where we might live. Elliot and Boyton, estate agents in Wigmore Street, showed me a small, newly-constructed block in Harley Street. Individual flats were being sold on long leases and garages were available in the mews. The block was near the Regent's Park end of Harley Street and had been built on the site of two Georgian houses, bombed in the Blitz, one of which had been Dr O'Donovan's. Normally, it was the practice of consultants to rent rooms from owners of the large Harley Street houses. Quite a number of doctors would consult from one house, hence the many name-plates on the front door, but their homes were elsewhere. However, we considered that, if we moved into Harley Street, Mick might pursue a small private practice from the flat as provided for in the lease of the superior landlord, the Howard de Walden Estate. We, therefore, purchased Flat 12, on the fifth floor by means of a mortgage from the Midland Bank. The apartment was made to look attractive. We had a consulting room (doubling up to serve as Mick's study), a small waiting-room and in the square entrance hall a desk was placed where I could receive the patients.

Sir Zachary Cope, one of Mick's chiefs when he was a student at St. Mary's, wrote a doggerel, the first verse of which read:

"Who has not heard of Harley Street
Where lots of doctors you will meet
All full of eagerness I guess
To climb the ladder of success?"

Chapter 17

Practice in Harley Street

The move from the spacious bungalow with a garden and friendly neighbours to a small apartment in the centre of town initially filled me with gloom. Only Kimmie, our talkative budgerigar, seemed unperturbed and chirpy as ever. He continued to recite his South London Tulse Hill telephone number and ignored that he now belonged to Welbeck.

I was fifty years old and had become nurse, receptionist, secretary, accountant, manager and general dogsbody to Mick's private practice. This grew steadily and, when the influx of Middle East patients began in the seventies, we became very busy. However, as a teaching hospital consultant, Mick gave his NHS work absolute priority. Being also a housewife, I had to leave the apartment at times to do essential shopping and the telephone was occasionally unmanned. Neither a telephone answering service nor machine proved entirely satisfactory — in the sixties people were not yet familiar with them. Marylebone High Street, with shops catering for almost everything and still a street of some character, was close at hand so I never needed to be out for long during the day.

London had became a centre for visitors. Our patients came from all over the world. I soon realised that people were essentially the same whatever their ethnic and cultural differences. I had no difficulties in dealing with the diversity of patients (though stumbling at times over some of the complicated names). Those who did not speak English usually brought an interpreter. Moslem women sometimes were unwilling to be fully examined. Many celebrities from the world of film, stage and television whom we saw, are still making headlines today.

In my capacity of nurse I carried out the treatment prescribed and assisted at minor surgery. I tried hard to do my best for the patients and to befriend them, especially those whose troubles were serious. Some skin disorders are not only disabling, disfiguring, painful or irritating, but may be chronic and recurrent. They can be life threatening. Sometimes they are a manifestation of serious internal disorder. Happily it was a time of medical advances and much more could be done for the individual case.

Some patients in turn befriended us. One was an elderly lady, Mrs Claude Beddington, she belonged to the Anglo-Irish gentry. In her time she had been an Edwardian beauty and had known many members of the aristocracy of that period. In 1929 her memoirs were published under the title *"All That I Have Met"*. For some reason, perhaps because we were rather slim, she felt that Mick and I were under-nourished, (which we were not) and arranged for Selfridges to send us food parcels from time to time.

One of our early patients was an Egyptian suffering from a widespread skin disorder for which Mick advised admission to hospital or nursing home. Owing to business commitments the patient declared this to be impossible, but he was prepared to attend daily for treatment. I applied ointments and dressings to most of his body surface, a laborious task because he was grossly obese. The results were striking. Within a few days his skin had cleared. The patient was so pleased and recommended fellow Egyptians to seek Mick's advice. One, I remember, was the mother of ex-King Farouk. The visits of such upper-class Egyptians ceased abruptly. President Nasser had confiscated their lands and money and they could no longer travel outside Egypt. Some years later, the wife of President Nasser's private secretary consulted Mick. Unfortunately, she was suffering from a potentially lethal disorder. On her return home she sent me sweets and an Egyptian-style ornamental gilt necklace and matching bracelet. In my evening classes I had sculptured a female head bearing some resemblance to that of Queen Nefertiti. I placed the necklace round its neck and it remains there still.

Members of the Arsenal football team in the year they won the Cup and were top of the First Division came to us, sent by Mr Street, their well-known physiotherapist. Their captain — was his name McLintock? — made a generous offer for our flat, although we had no intention to sell. I remember the tone of excitement in the voice of an Iranian patient when he recognised in the waiting room the Arsenal player who scored the winning goal in the Cup Final. "Isn't that Charlie George?" Our footballers clearly had a good reputation in Tehran, but that was before the days of the Ayatollahs.

Mr Paul Getty, the oil magnate, reputed to be the richest man on earth, paid us three guineas, then our usual consultation fee. Sometime previously we had visited Sutton Place, a tudor mansion in Surrey, then Mr Getty's home where we were able to view his fine collection of paintings and books, the basis later of Paul Getty museum of California. Another patient was Dr Mannie Otaba, oil minister of the United Arab Emirates and head of Opec who had great personal charm. He came with two young men who bulged under their jackets; presumably they were bodyguards carrying firearms. On another occasion several members of the Royal Family from Abu Dhabi had booked successive appointments. No-one turned up and Mick and I sat twiddling our thumbs. Hardly surprising for it was Ascot Week.

In the course of my work I did a considerable amount of typing. General practitioners received letters advising them on the diagnosis and treatment of their patients. Solicitors required reports on dermatitis of possible occupational origin. Mick was writing articles for the medical press on a variety of dermatological subjects. The drug companies were producing new, more powerful steroid creams for the treatment of common skin disorders like eczema or psoriasis. Mick and his colleagues at St. Mary's were engaged in clinical research evaluating possible side-effects from absorption of steroids through the skin into the general circulation, when such potent creams were applied extensively or for a prolonged period. Papers were prepared reporting the results for publication in medical journals like the *Lancet*. The Ministry of Health now requires containers of steroid creams to carry cautionary advice as to their use especially in young children.

When I married Mick I hoped to be able to assist him in his work. Our years in Harley Street fulfilled this expectation. However, my first action of support was to cheer him from the touch-line of the Rugby football field when he played for the Old Paulines. After the match I helped in the Pavilion. Carrying a tray of tea cups I walked through a door only to be confronted by a group of naked men splashing about in a communal bath and singing at the top of their voices. Nearly dropping the tray, I beat a hasty retreat.

During the War when Mick was serving in Persia, he sent me a letter describing a game of Rugby football between a Rhodesian Air Squadron and a team from the British Army in which he was included. This was played on a hard, stony field almost devoid of grass in a mountainous region of Persia. The Rhodesians being such good athletes easily beat the army side. It was to be Mick's last game of Rugby football.

Chapter 18

Painting and Other Activities

In the course of my studies as a nurse I had enjoyed drawing and sketching to illustrate my lecture notes. Mick came across some of my old notebooks and, impressed by my efforts, suggested I approach Mrs Connie Dyson, then Principal of Hillcroft College, to permit me to attend the art classes. This she did and so I learnt something about paints, canvases, brushes, palettes and composition and began painting at home. Like many other people, I found the pastime completely absorbing and the new hobby was to be my stand-by for very many years.

When we moved to Harley Street I attended in the evenings various short art courses including those at St. Martin's School of Art and the London Polytechnic where I also took a few tentative steps in sculpture. Then I joined the City Literary Institute (City Lit) art classes. The Institute held a summer vacation course at Bishop Otter Training College for Teachers in Chichester. For Mick also to come he, as a non-student, had to satisfy the tutors of competence in his chosen subject. He toyed with the Russian novel but plumped for *"History of England in the Middle Ages"*. After an interview in which he was asked fairly searching questions he was accepted. Perhaps it was felt useful to have a doctor around. He was in fact busy at times coping with minor accidents.

We both enjoyed the courses. I was free to paint all day under the watchful eye of the Art Tutor. Mick worked late into the night studying textbooks and writing essays. Remembering my Hillcroft days I sympathised with him. He became quite erudite on topics such as "The State of the Crafts in the Reign of Henry II". Bishop Otter College is ideal as a centre for vacation studies. It has extensive grounds stretching as far as St. Richard's Hospital. In our free time we visited the Festival Theatre and saw Shaw's 'St. Joan' with Joan Plowright and Chekov's 'Uncle Vanya' with Lord

Olivier. We toured the cathedral and city walls, visited Petworth House with its famous park, fine carvings by Grindley Gibbons, old masters and the many Turners, painted by the artist while a guest at the house.

Later Mick and I attended a painting holiday organised by the magazine, *The Artist*. We travelled on the car ferry from Boulogne to Avignon and drove on into the village of Aigaliers in Provence. The painting group had their meals in the local auberge and slept in the Presbytery and dispersed round the village and its environs to find suitable subjects for painting. Under the guidance of the tutors, Charles Bone and Peter Garrard, we went on excursions to nearby beauty spots such as the Pont du Gard and Nîmes with its Greek temple, the Maison Carré. Some of my paintings from this holiday such as "The Silk Farm" now hang on the walls of our Bournemouth flat and provide many pleasant memories.

We spent a painting holiday at the Mountain Studio near the Brecon Beacons in Wales. We stayed at the Gliffaes Hotel on the river bank of the beautiful Usk; popular with anglers. I remember standing by the river, seeing the sudden blue flash of a kingfisher; also the still waters of the reservoirs in the nearby Brecon National Park. These were surrounded by woods of Forestry Commission conifers, unfortunately almost devoid of birds or other wildlife. At Crickhowell is an ancient bridge with very many spans over the Usk. Near Tallybont, as one looks in an upward direction, colourful long-boat pleasure craft glide past silently; the canal is at a higher level than the countryside. To the north are the Sugar Loaf and Table Mountains and, behind them, the Black Mountains. Altogether this is splendid scenery and ideal for painting.

Another year we went to Coubertou near Cahors in the Lot region of Southern France where Peter Norton ran his painting holiday. The Lot is an area of small farms, comprising a field of maize, a vineyard, a few head of cattle, some free-ranging poultry and a vegetable plot; rather different from our English "prairie" farms of today. Peter Norton attracted some very proficient painters and I felt humble in comparison.

In 1967, after the International Congress of Dermatology at Munich, Mick and I hired a cottage by the Staffelsee in Upper Bavaria and there I painted a view of the lake. This picture was submitted to the Housewife's Painting Competition organised by *The Times*. The late Dame Laura Knight was one of the judges. It was selected for hanging in the Grosvenor Galleries. My paintings have also been hung in the Ben Uri Gallery and Mall Gallery in Carlton House Terrace. A painting of anemones hangs in the consulting room of a dermatologist friend in Dallas; another, of daffodils, is in a flat of a Guy's physician in Harley House.

My largest painting depicts the monk Gregor Mendel holding in his hand a pointer. He is demonstrating the laws of heredity, which he established in the middle of the last century. The figure of Mendel is surrounded by flowering garden peas, the plant on which he made his original observations. The middle of the painting consists of the earth's sphere. Superimposed on the earth is a circle of cells in the phases of division and illustrating the separation of the chromosomes. Towards the left side of the picture is the Watson and Crick double helix of DNA beginning to unfold and replicate. I call this painting 'Inheritance'.

When the BBC produced a programme on Mendel and his research called 'The Garden of Inheritance' I sent them a colour photograph of my painting and received back a nice letter from the producer praising the manner in which I caught the monk's expression and demonstrated the impact of his discoveries.

In 1969 before the days of purpose-built conference halls, it was my lot, acting for Mick, to make the administrative arrangements for the Annual Meeting for the British Association of Dermatologists taking place in London under the presidency of Dr G. B. Mitchell-Heggs of St. Mary's Hospital. I had to make do on a financial shoe-string (registration fee was only £1.1s). The main venue for the meeting, where the lectures and the Annual Dinner took place, was the Royal College of Physicians, a fine modern building designed by Sir Dennis Lasdun, which blends in with the neighbouring Regency Nash terraces. The President's reception was held in Chandos House, an eighteenth century Robert Adam residence in Queen Anne Street.

About five hundred guests sat down to the dinner. The caterers were Messrs Ring and Brymer who supplied and served the selected menus and wines. I had garlanded the tables in blue, the colours of St. Mary's and placed an arrangement of cornflowers on each table. On one afternoon some members played golf in the Old Deer Park, Richmond, others sailed on the Welsh Harp; whilst another party of members and their wives went on an excursion by coach to Hatfield House, the stately Jacobean home in Hertfordshire built by Robert Cecil, the first Earl of Salisbury, teas being served in the Old Palace. The Cecil family also own Cranborne Manor not too far from Bournemouth, to which is attached a small garden centre. There, some ten years ago, I bought a seedling Parlour Palm, *Chamaedorea elegans* which has now grown to a respectable size. On the final morning of the meeting a demonstration of patients took place at St. Mary's Hospital in Paddington.

F

On the basis of the invalid cookery I learnt as part of my nurses' training, I enlarged my experience in cooking. During the war I saved on my rations, baked several cakes and sent them by post to Mick stationed in the desert near Basra, the Iraqui port town. In his letter, Mick described the delight and pleasure these cakes gave the troops when they all arrived within a few days in time for Christmas 1942. I continued making cakes, mince pies and boxes of sweets for the various hospitals until it came to Mick's retirement. "Penny's mince pies" establishing something of a reputation. We had an American friend who used to fly over from California just to sample my "cookies". This was not true, of course, he just said it to please me. One day we learnt that he had been murdered. Unless violence strikes at someone close, its impact is not fully felt. We miss our friend very much.

I like entertaining and dispensing hospitality. Mick and I started giving parties soon after rationing ended. Our Streatham Hill bungalow was very suitable for large gatherings and I organised a treasure-hunt when we entertained members of the Dowling Club, a group of young dermatologists and their wives.

Dr Geoffrey Dowling who founded the travel and journal club which held monthly meetings in the George Inn, Southwark, was a beloved figure amongst aspiring dermatologists. They valued his advice and were encouraged by his enthusiasm. His daughter, Jane Dowling, is a well-known artist.

Although it was small, many guests could be accommodated in our Harley Street flat. When Mick was Chairman of the St. Mary's Gazette Committee we entertained the students who had been involved in the production of the *Gazette* over the past years. In the event, about seventy students sat down to the evening meal. I was not caught short on the food but we had to send out a party to replenish the drinks. The thirst of the St. Mary's students is proverbial, which may be connected with their prowess at Rugby football.

When St. Mary's Hospital, Praed Street and Paddington General Hospital in Harrow Road were about to form a joint unit, Mick and I thought it a good idea to give what we called an engagement party for the consultants of both hospitals to bring them closer together. This turned out to be a great success and lasted until the early hours of the morning.

One member of this union, Paddington General Hospital, has now been closed. When a hospital which has served a community for a long time is shut down the loss may be deeply felt. Certainly Paddington General Hospital, though held in high esteem, was structurally an old decrepit building that had evolved from the infirmary and workhouse of one hundred years ago. To compensate for the closure of the hospital a new wing, the Queen Elizabeth, the Queen Mother Wing, incorporating the latest technical aids and advances, has been built at St. Mary's Hospital overlooking the Regent's canal basin.

The Annual Dinner of the St. John's Hospital Dermatological Society is preceded by an oration. While the men are attending this lecture, their ladies are obliged to wait around until it ends. So I invited them to the Harley Street flat for refreshments until it was time to rejoin the husbands for the dinner at the Royal College of Physicians, having previously hired a coach for the short return journey to the college. The Ladies' Party went exceedingly well, everyone became quite merry and we lost all sense of time. Finally we were interrupted by knocking on the door of the flat. The coach driver said he had been waiting half an hour, what had become of us? Hastily we donned our wraps and were driven to the college. We had struck a blow for feminism, the men for a change, and not the ladies, had been kept waiting and were hungry and thirsty. However, all was forgiven over the subsequent excellent meal.

Chapter 19

Tales Not Yet Told

I had a friend, Kay Hopkins, who possessed outstanding good looks with striking blonde hair. Before her marriage she had been a nurse at St. Mary's Hospital. From time to time, Kay would mention her older sister Jill who worked for Archibald McIndoe, but I never met her. The outstanding achievements throughout the war of the special plastic unit under the direction of Archibald McIndoe at the Victoria Hospital, East Grinstead, became widely recognised. The unit had won a reputation for spectacular reconstructive surgery on behalf of the very many servicemen injured or burnt in action. The patients of Ward Three became the 'Guinea Pig Club' who after the war kept in touch with one another and returned to East Grinstead for reunions.

Jill, like her sister Kay, was apparently a beauty with Titian-like red hair. The vivacious Jill was McIndoe's theatre sister and was constantly by his side. She also shared his very active social life and was a valued guest, as his companion, at gatherings of the local Sussex gentry. McIndoe's wife and children during the war years were in America. After the war he returned to the London Clinic in Harley Street to resume his flourishing private practice; Jill joined him there as his theatre nurse and assistant.

When McIndoe was divorced by his wife, Jill fully expected to marry him. They had, after all, been closely associated for twenty-two years. However, Sir Archibald chose a younger woman as the new Lady McIndoe.

Eventually Jill married a South African businessman. He was a cousin of Mary, Mick's sister-in-law. Jill's story now ends sadly. When Jill Denton, as she had now become, was sailing to South Africa on the *City of Port Elizabeth*, she had a stroke and then a second which proved fatal. She was buried at sea. Jill was still relatively young. Sir Archibald, writing after her death, stated "that to work with her was pure joy".

During the war I briefly met the sister of Richard Hillary who was a Spitfire pilot destroying several German planes until he himself was brought down in flames. He was a patient in Ward Three at East Grinstead and underwent many painful operations to correct facial injuries and those to his hands. He wrote *"The Last Enemy"* graphically describing his experiences. Unfortunately, Hillary crashed later when he was allowed to resume night flying and was killed, as was his navigator. Great interest was aroused recently, when a series of love-letters were found, which he had written to a beautiful, but older woman. Extracts from these letters revealed a moving and stirring romance.

When Sir Archibald, troubled by a diseased gall bladder, had to have it removed, he chose the well-known St. Mary's Surgeon, Mr Arthur Dickson Wright for the operation. 'Dickie' as he was called, was a phenomenal worker. At one time few families in North West London did not have some member on whom Dickie had operated. Like Margaret Thatcher, he required very little sleep and took catnaps when the occasion offered. He was in great demand as an after-dinner speaker, although not everyone appreciated his stories.

After the injuries I had received in Spain, which I have already mentioned, surgical intervention again became necessary and Mr Dickson Wright proceeded to deal with me in the Lindo Wing. During one of his rounds, Dickie apparently disappeared. Sister, becoming aware of his absence went to look for him. When she entered my room, she found Dickie asleep in an armchair, while I was likewise asleep in my bed! Dickie was taking a catnap, but this one was lasting a little longer than usual.

When we moved into Harley Street, the resident caretaker used to take the rubbish bins from the flats down in the passenger lift for emptying. Nothing wrong in that, but the hour for rubbish collecting appeared to get later and later, even after nine o'clock in the morning. I felt this to be wrong and made my opinion clear to the caretaker, no rubbish bin should be carried in the lift after eight o'clock. However, this created tension, for the caretaker's instructions were given by the landlord's manager — not by a flat owner like myself

The landlords were Hammerson, a property company which has been in the news recently because of the finding of relics of unique Roman baths at the City site where they are developing a new office-block. As I had a few shares in Hammerson I went along to the Annual General Meeting held in their sumptuous Park Lane Head Office. Before the meeting began, shareholders were offered sherry and canapés and mingled with the directors. I found myself with a group in which the Chairman, Sidney Mason, was in conversation with another member of the Company. I expected they would be discussing matters of high finance, but no — the subject was rubbish bins in passenger lifts in their Harley Street property and the opposition of one lady resident to their presence in the lift after eight o'clock! What was the upshot? Bins were collected much earlier — and Hammerson sold the block of flats to another landlord.

The actress Eleanor Bron lived in the flat above us in Harley Street. She liked riding a bicycle even in the traffic-ridden West End and took cycling holidays on the continent. However, it is not about her cycling activities I want to tell. We never heard a sound from Eleanor's flat above, except on very rare occasions. Then, possibly after a theatre performance, we might, in the early hours of the morning, be woken by the sound of singing and playing on the piano. The flats have common air vents and, in the quiet of the night, noise was exaggerated. I would knock on the ceiling with a broomstick until peace and quiet were restored and I could resume my sleep!

One day, the *Evening Standard* published a glowing review of a performance by Eleanor. Mick cut it out and, in case she had not seen it, slipped it through her letter-box. Later, there was a ring at our door. Eleanor stood outside "What have I done now?" she asked "What are your complaints?" She pointed to Mick's scribbling in a typical doctor's handwriting; for 'with compliments' one could easily read 'with complaints'.

In 1976, I accompanied my husband to the Old Bailey when he gave evidence at the trial of the Maguire family. They were charged with making bombs for the IRA with which to blow up the public house in Guildford and were found guilty.

Mrs Annie Maguire was the aunt of Mr Conlan one of the "Guildford four" charged with the bombing and convicted. He under pressure implicated the Maguire household as being a bomb factory. When the police with sniffer dogs raided the Maguire home no traces of explosive were found. However, scrapings were taken from hands and finger-nails of the Maguires and the forensic laboratory reported that most of the specimens gave positive chemical identification for nitro-glycerine. On this forensic evidence the Maguires were convicted and sentenced to very long terms of imprisonment; although protesting their innocence.

Mrs Annie Maguire had been a patient of Mick's at St. Mary's Hospital. She was suffering from dermatitis of the hands due to washing-up activities and he had prescribed steroid cream and the wearing of polythene gloves to protect her hands. Mick was in the witness-box for only a couple of minutes. After the verdict of guilty he told me that judging by Mrs Maguire's demeanour during visits to the hospital, she was, in his opinion, innocent of the alleged crimes. The nursing staff of the out-patient department and her general practitioner likewise considered Mrs Maguire not guilty.

Some years later, a 'Panorama' programme on the BBC pointed to the possibility of a miscarriage of justice over the Maguires. Mick wrote to the presenter of the programme, I believe it was Mr Robert Kee, suggesting that the tests which demonstrated nitro-glycerine in scrapings from fingers had given false positive results due to cross-reactions with other substances, possibly derived from wearing polythene gloves.

The position now is that the 'Guildford four' have been declared innocent and the forensic evidence incriminating the Maguire family has been found "unsafe". Having served long prison sentences, the Maguires are now at last free and exonerated.

Professor Herman Beerman of Philadelphia and his wife are our very good friends. He is a distinguished doyen of American dermatology. When they visited us in Bournemouth, we took them on excursions into the countryside including the New Forest and Corfe Castle. In the village of Minstead (about which I have already written) we went to the old church and then into the churchyard to see the grave of Sir Arthur Conan Doyle and his wife. It made Herman's day. He is a keen member of the Copper Beeches, the Philadelphia Society of Holmes enthusiasts, and has written about Holmes's many allusions to dermatology. However, Mick was able to inform Herman about something quite unknown to the dermatological fans of Sherlock Holmes. Sir Malcolm Morris was the first consultant dermatologist of St. Mary's and moved to Harley Street in the 1880s. His son relates how Dr Arthur Conan Doyle, then a general practitioner, brought a patient to see him and subsequently Morris and Conan Doyle became close friends. It was apparently Morris, who, after reading 'A Study in Scarlet', followed by 'The Sign of Four', advised Conan Doyle to abandon his medical practice and devote himself to literature and Sherlock Holmes. One day Conan Doyle asked Morris to indicate a suitable part of London where Sherlock Holmes should reside. Morris mentioned 21 Baker Street, where his grandfather had lived after he retired from the Bombay Civil Service. He was able to lay his hands on the particulars of sale of 21 Baker Street prepared by order of the executors of his grandfather (John Morris) in 1840. Conan Doyle modified this plan of the house to suit his idea for the requirements of Holmes, Dr Watson and Mrs Hudson. 21 Baker Street was however, a private house so Conan Doyle invented 221B to avoid possible trouble with owners of No 21. If there ever was a 221B, it would have been on the site now occupied by the offices of the Abbey National Building Society. The Building Society still receives many letters addressed to Sherlock Holmes at 221B Baker Street and they acknowledge such letters.

Part V

'And to Make an End is to Make a Beginning'

Chapter 20

Aftermath

After Mick's retirement as consultant dermatologist to St. Mary's, he remained on as sub-Dean for Postgraduate Studies for a while and when this appointment came to an end, we decided to leave Harley Street for Bournemouth, because my eyes were beginning to give trouble. We had been in Harley Street for nearly twenty years. I had enjoyed the work and contact with so many interesting personalities — a microcosm of the world to which I have already alluded. We sold the flat to a colleague, a dermatologist at University College Hospital, in order that patients should have continuing care when requiring an appointment.

On the day following our move to Bournemouth, the doorbell rang. An Arab dressed in white robes had arrived who had obtained our new address from the Harley Street caretaker. I then recalled a telephone conversation on the day before we departed with a man requesting an urgent appointment. The speaker sounded very clear, as if he was in the vicinity. I explained that we were leaving London at noon the next day, but the caller insisted on seeing Mick, although I offered him the name of another dermatologist. I then said, "If you can be in Harley Street by 11.30 a.m., doctor will see you". He did not arrive and off we went — but now he was here in Bournemouth. I enquired why he had not kept his appointment and he replied "My plane was late". I could hardly credit that the phone call had been made from the Gulf because of its clarity. After his consultation with Mick the patient returned to Heathrow and flew back the same day to Abu Dhabi. Our professional life had ended.

Many years previously, while we were holidaying in the South of France, we passed through Cannes. I remember it being a particularly bright sunny day. Suddenly, on the beach, I experienced severe pain in both eyes and could not tolerate the light. We hurried to find a shop which sold sun-glasses. From that day I have suffered from photo-sensitivity. Years later, when I began to develop central vision cataracts and some degeneration of the retina, I put this down to the damage produced by excessive ultraviolet radiation sustained at Cannes.

The mist over my eyes increased, and in September 1979, Sir Stephen Miller, ophthalmologist to the Queen, who had a flat below us when we lived in Harley Street, operated on me for removal of cataracts. I was in King Edward VII Hospital in Beaumont Street at the time when Lord and Lady Brabourne, were also patients. They had been injured as a result of a bomb attack in Ireland on their boat in which Lady Brabourne's father, Lord Mountbatten, her son Nicholas and a young friend were killed.

As I have sustained damage to the retina my sight is very limited and it took a long time to adjust. However, I now bump less often into obstacles and on the whole I do get by, wearing dark thick glasses. Today implants of plastic lenses into the eyes after cataract extraction have transformed the lives of patients who have no need to wear spectacles except, perhaps, for reading and who retain full fields of vision.

In King Edward VII Hospital, following the eye operations, matron brought into my room a talking-book machine and tape of George Eliot's *'The Mill on the Floss'*. I wept at the story, but delighted in the new world that had opened up. Ever since, and it is now for many years, I have listened to the tapes sent to me through the Royal National Institute for the Blind, who also supplied the talking-book machine. The books come in special cassettes of complete stories. I have now listened to a whole range of classical novels, historical romances, biographies and thrillers. I like John Le Carré and feel I know more about espionage than Peter Wright ever did.

Talking-books are also available in standard audio cassettes. These are supplied by 'Calibre', a charitable organisation. In addition, a Bournemouth Community Centre sends me a Talking Newspaper of local events, and the ladies from the nearby library also bring me cassettes, a service I appreciate very much. So while I do my chores, I can listen to tales of murder, assassination and evil conspiracy, worlds without end.

When he was sixty-nine years old, my husband suffered an influenza-like illness which showed no signs of abating. He was found to have subacute bacterial endocarditis, a streptococcal infection of one of the heart valves. He was admitted to the intensive care unit at the Lansdowne Hospital in Bournemouth and received large doses of intravenous penicillin by continuous drip for over two weeks. I was permitted to assist in his nursing which Mick appreciated.

Subacute bacterial endocarditis, which, as I remember from my hospital days, was then invariably fatal, is now, thanks to penicillin, eminently treatable and Mick too made a good recovery. Every time he goes for a dental check-up he takes a prophylactic dose of penicillin because organisms, which live harmlessly on the gums, may be dispersed during dental procedures into the bloodstream and settle on heart valves, causing endocarditis.

Mick related to me that in 1935 he and his fellow students at St. Mary's attended Professor Alexander Fleming's lectures on microbiology delivered in a broad Scots' accent. Fleming told of his search for antibacterial agents. In 1928 he had shown (and this is now part of British history) that a substance, which he called penicillin, derived from a mould, possessed antibacterial activity. Mick remembers Fleming as a dour but very pleasant and easy-going personality with a twinkle in his blue eyes and an inevitable cigarette dangling from the corner of his mouth. He was a keen rifle shot, liked snooker and organised parties to the Chelsea Arts Ball. In the laboratory he was an immaculate worker and no-one equalled his technical skills. After the death of his first wife, Fleming married Amelia, a Greek bacteriologist who had become his assistant. Later, when Fleming had died, she returned to Greece but was maltreated by the Greek colonels who ruled at that time. In 1981, St. Mary's celebrated the centenary of Fleming's birth and Lady Fleming was able to attend. A blue plaque was unveiled on his old Chelsea home. Mick who had just been cured of a potentially lethal infection by the wonder drug was present at this gathering, which took place nearly fifty years after he had heard Fleming's lecture on the discovery of penicillin. A story goes that, when Sir Alexander Fleming toured the Jerez region of Southern Spain, he visited a bodega. On a barrel he saw an inscription which read "Penicillin cures the sick, but a glass of sherry awakens the dead."

Sir Alexander Fleming's Nobel Prize medallions and others recently came up for auction. Luckily, Fleming's son, a general practitoner, was able to secure them for the family.

Chapter 21

The Family Leaves Tottenham
and Broadwater Farm

Today Tottenham would be called an 'inner city area'. However, it is a fair distance from Central London and came about as part of London's Victorian urban sprawl towards the north-east and the valley of the River Lea. After I left home in my teens, my parents, grandparents, uncles and aunts, continued to live in Tottenham. Gradually, my brothers and sisters began to disperse after a land-mine dropped in Stamford Road during the war destroying our house amongst many others.

A year or two after World War II, my father, now in his late seventies, became ill; his heart was failing. I made arrangements for him to be brought by ambulance to our bungalow in Streatham Hill where I nursed him in his final days. I was very fond of my father. All his life he had worked extremely hard on jobs which are now performed by machines. His day usually began about five in the morning when he would carry out numerous chores in and about the house, all the while singing or humming to himself before setting out to work or to queue up at the employment exchange. As I previously mentioned, my father never struck us children. If my mother asked him to chastise us because of some misdemeanour he would half raise his hand as if to strike a blow, spluttering "I'll, I'll — throw half-a-crown at you, if you don't behave yourself" and at that we would relax, the crisis being over.

After my father died, my mother lived with my elder sister Violet in a small house in Fawley Road, Tottenham, just opposite Gestetner's, manufacturers of office equipment, where Violet worked. She now led a tranquil life. Occasionally she would come and stay with me for a few weeks. When she was eighty-five years old, Mother and Violet went on a coach trip to Scotland. Mick and I waited for them on their return at the coach terminus. I was a little apprehensive expecting Mother to be exhausted, but she was in good fettle after the exciting time she had experienced. When nearly ninety, Mother became ill and was admitted to St. Ann's Hospital in Tottenham. As she was somewhat confused during her illness, the doctors wanted to transfer her to Claybury Mental Hospital in Essex; at this I demurred but had great difficulty in finding a suitable private nursing home where she remained until she died.

After Mother died, the Tottenham Council, anxious to demolish the house in Fawley Road for road widening, placed my sister Violet into a one-bedroom flat in a large block on their new huge residential complex, the Broadwater Farm Estate. This was constructed in the early seventies and the architect won a prize for its design. (I remember my mother telling me that when she was a young girl there was a large farm with adjoining marshland at that site). The interior of Violet's flat was quite pleasant. It had constant hot water, central heating and at the back a cheerful outlook over green fields and a stream.

The Broadwater Farm Estate consists of massive concrete tower blocks of varying heights. Walkways, open to wind and rain, bring occupants from stairs and lifts to their flats. There are over one thousand "units of accommodation" which is the term used by the housing authorities. Seen from a distance or on television, where it has been featured quite frequently, the silhouette of the Estate is impressive as it stands out, Manhattan-like, from the surroundings. For its inhabitants it is a concrete jungle, although some have tried to soften the harsh impact with pots of geraniums or other plants on ground-floor patios. It is situated some distance from the high street shops, buses and the underground, and likewise is rather far from factories and other places of employment. Hopefully, in the future, deregulation of buses will bring minibuses right into the Estate as most of its people do not own cars.

Many occupants of the Estate, young and one-parent families, the old, and very old, the widowed, the disabled, the unemployed and the very many blacks, rely on the DSS for a proportion or all of their income and cost of living.

When I first visited my sister Violet in the Broadwater Farm, there seemed to be little communal activity. I noticed a small supermarket and the office of the Housing Authority which was closed. Boys were riding on their bicycles but there did not appear to be much in the way of amenities for young children or the old. When Violet first lived on the Estate she frequently complained about mugging of elderly residents and the unpleasant smells in the lifts and stairways. She became friendly with a neighbour and after some time her adverse comments practically ceased. "What has happened to the muggings?" I asked. "Oh, the boys have grown up", Violet replied. She had settled down and was enjoying the comfort of the flat. Meanwhile through the initiative of the spirited lady, a Youth Association was formed. Princess Diana came to the opening of its premises and this was shown on television.

In 1985, riots occurred in which PC Blakelock was brutally murdered. Since then an effort has been made to develop more communal enterprises. The Estate is being renovated and a memorial garden for PC Blakelock and Mrs Cynthia Jarrett, whose death sparked off the riots, has been constructed. Recently a drug-smuggling ring was uncovered in 'Debden', the block of the Estate in which my sister Violet lived.

Shortly after we had moved to Bournemouth, Violet's neighbour, who had become her friend, died suddenly and Violet, now over eighty, began to show signs of senility. She became forgetful, particularly of recent events, repetitive, asking the same question over and over again, and showed increasing tendency to make mistakes such as putting a kettle on the turned-on gas without igniting it, and becoming confused as to where she was. My husband and I consulted her doctor who pronounced the Broadwater Farm to be a death-trap for the aged and advised that Violet should not be allowed to live alone. We, therefore, made arrangements for her to enter Balholm Grange, a private rest-home, for two weeks as a guest. Eventually, after this initial try-out, she was persuaded to become a resident.

Balholm Grange is situated in the pine-scented district of Branksome Park, Poole. What a change of scene from Tottenham! It has now become a registered nursing home with qualified staff, and Violet has been there for over six years. As regards her maintenance Violet contributes from her occupational pension scheme and with an Attendance Allowance and DSS Allowance her fees are almost covered. Such help from Social Security was not available when it was necessary for my mother to enter a home.

Taking an elderly person from their customary environment is hazardous. Confusion and difficulties may increase. Senile dementia or Alzheimer's Disease is common and few of us will escape it occurring in some member of our families or in friends.

Violet was the last of my brothers and sisters to leave Tottenham. The small houses in the vicinity where I grew up have mostly disappeared or come into private ownership, thanks to the availability of mortgages. They have been spruced up and now represent a considerable capital asset to their owners.

Chapter 22

Travellers' Joys

Specialists in their various fields of medicine frequently visit centres at home and abroad to attend meetings, conferences and congresses, so as to keep abreast of advances and to fraternise with their colleagues. Wives are usually invited to join their husbands and are catered for in ladies' programmes. Some of the experiences when accompanying my husband have particularly remained in my mind.

An early visit was to a meeting in Vienna. I much enjoyed the sensation of speeding along the autobahn. During the stay in Vienna our group of English dermatologists had lunch in the restaurant situated in the basement of the town hall, the Rathauskeller. After the meal we made for a taxi parked nearby, got into the taxi and gave the driver our destination. To our consternation, the taxi sped off at a furious pace, driving over lawns and even low railings of an adjoining park in an erratic and completely random manner. Though we did not know it at the time, we had woken the taxi-driver from a drunken torpor; he had no idea where he was going or what he was doing and our lives were in his hands. He then drove out of the park into the main street, missing trams and cars by inches as they bore down on us. Suddenly, and for no apparent reason, the driver stopped his vehicle and we tumbled out as quickly as we could.

Another occasion concerned Kimmie, my blue and white budgerigar. He was a great talker with a good vocabulary and I was very fond of him. Mick and I were due to attend a meeting in Nantes. I was loath to leave Kimmie behind, but France had strictly prohibited all importation of parakeets for fear of psittacosis. However, a newspaper carried a report that Sir Winston Churchill had a special dispensation allowing him to take his pet budgerigar (which was fond of perching on his head) into France. So I wrote to the French Ambassador in London pleading that Kimmie too be permitted to enter France. Eventually a letter arrived from Paris. Providing Kimmie had a clean bill of health from a veterinary surgeon he would be allowed into France. On arrival by car in Boulogne we were unwise enough to show Kimmie in his cage to the Customs Officer; even after perusal of the letters and health certificate, the official remained reluctant to let him in. Instead he led us to what presumably were the offices of the Boulogne Department of Veterinary Medicine housed in an old musty building, a sort of museum full of stuffed animals and birds; these had probably been brought back by French explorers many centuries ago. We were interviewed by another official of superior rank, who again studied the documents in disbelief that the rigid regulations concerning parakeets were to be breached. Finally Kimmie was allowed into France.

On arrival at the hotel in Nantes we left Kimmie with reception while we went to our allotted room to unpack. When the English dermatologists checked in, they were very surprised to be greeted by ''Good afternoon doctor, would you like a cup of tea or glass of sherry?'' Later Kimmie learnt to say *''Je suis un petit inseparable''*. He was a great social success, and colleagues, both French and English, continued to enquire after him for many years.

Sometimes a holiday or foreign tour followed a conference. Twenty-five years ago Mick and I attended a conference in Miami Beach. We could not swim in the sea (the Americans call it the ocean) because it was dense with Portuguese men-of-war. After the meeting we flew on to New Orleans, wandered down Bourbon Street (unlike Alistair Cook I know little about the Blues) and round the French Quarter, and sauntered along Canal Street to the Mississippi Basin and its Show Boats. We also took a coach tour with the Gray Line. The guide in his Southern drawl told us about the Louisiana purchase and battles which were quite mysterious to me. We passed a huge cemetery where the dead were laid to rest above the ground. Mick visited the skin department of both Louisiana and Tulane University Hospitals. He had to be there before eight o'clock in the morning; the Americans start early. His guide was Dr Jolly of Baton Rouge some distance away who always rose at 5 a.m. to start his working day — or so he told us.

Leaving New Orleans we moved on to Mexico City; it was Christmas time and the decorations in the street and parks were out of this world. However, the city was noisy and cold, snow falling for the first time in its history, I was told; nor did I feel too well, my trouble was Montezuma's revenge (travellers' diarrhoea). It was the Spaniards under Cortez who killed the Aztecs and their king, and it seemed unfair of Montezuma to take revenge on an English woman until I remembered I had once been a member of the Spanish Army! We took refuge on Cozumel, an island just off the coast of the Yucatan peninsula. I swam in the warm Caribbean sea, soon felt better and thoroughly enjoyed Cozumel's idyllic atmosphere. I had a favourite rocky ledge from which to enter the sea. One day a group of youths had gathered at my spot, gesticulating and pointing; apparently a very large octopus had its home under my ledge! I have a particular horror of these creatures. After Cozumel, we visited the remarkable Mayan remains at Uxmal and Chichen Itza. The Yucatan thus offers the holiday-maker both an ideal seaside and relics of a fascinating civilisation.

Before returning home via Washington DC we visited friends in Dallas. Altogether we had been on many aeroplanes, seen numerous places of interest and made lasting friends.

Hurricane Gilbert which did so much damage to the Caribbean area also struck Cozumel. May this Robinson Crusoe island of mine soon recover!

Some years later we again visited the United States for the meeting of the American Dermatological Association of which Mick had become an honorary member. The venue was in the Hotel del Coronado situated by the Pacific Ocean in San Diego, California. The in-house video informed us it was here that Edward, Prince of Wales, first met Mrs Simpson. Queuing for breakfast began at 6.30 a.m., but delicious strawberries served with the breakfast compensated for the delays. In the hotel arcade of shops and boutiques was one which offered to trace genealogies of those named Phelps amongst others. The ladies took a trip to Tijuana in Mexico and I had the opportunity to buy some souvenirs of the local handicrafts. After the meeting in San Diego we flew to Los Angeles and stayed in the Beverly Hills Hilton. Friends who lived in Bel-Air told us that at night deer came down from the hills into the garden and ate the hibiscus shrubs. Soon we were touring along the coastal highway towards San Francisco. The coach was very comfortable, the driver a splendid guide and our American fellow passengers charming. Stops were made at places with familiar names, San Simeon and Hearst Castle, Cartmel of Clint Eastwood fame and Monterey with its famous golf-course of Pebble Beach. The country of the giant redwoods, the tallest living trees on earth, was reached on the way to San Francisco. Here on Fisherman's Wharf, we found an Indonesian snack-bar that supplied breakfast of three eggs, sunny-side up, potato croquettes, toast and coffee ad lib, which set us up practically for the rest of the day at a reasonable price. San Francisco is reputed to be a gourmet's paradise so we queued at a much praised well-known fish restaurant, but when the precious course was finally served the fish was spoilt by being smothered in a thick sauce. Before the long flight home Mick spent one day at Stanford University's dermatology department.

Eight years ago, the International Congress of Dermatology, held in Tokyo, provided opportunity for touring the Far East. The New Otani Hotel had ample accommodation for the two thousand or more delegates. The congress dinner was a grand affair with Crown Prince, now Emperor, Achito and the Crown Princess present. After the meal, the hall was darkened to allow for a dazzling display of flashing laser beams. While talking to a young Japanese lady manning a stall in the drug companies' exhibition, I mentioned that I was unable to see sufficiently to apply make-up to my face for the evening dinner. Michiko, (for that was her name) immediately offered to do this for me which she did very skilfully. I invited Michiko to Bournemouth and she visited us some months later. We took her to Broadlands, the stately home of the Mountbatten family, now open to the public, where, as I have related, Mick was stationed early in the war.

Michiko has married an anatomist who works in University College so they now live in London and are part of the growing local Japanese community.

What one remembers about Japan is the cleanliness, the white gloves worn by the taxi-drivers, railway attendants and policemen or the hot moist towels supplied in the plane. Also the deer in the park at Nara, which given a biscuit bow politely, like their human counterparts.

In Hong Kong, the boy on our floor at the Mandarin Hotel greeted us by name. As visitors by the hundreds are in and out of the hotel daily, this feat of memory indicates the intelligence of the people who have made such a success of Hong Kong.

Bangkok and Thailand provided many new impressions such as the gentleness of the people and the very light touch which young children give as a sign that they had something to sell.

Two years later we planned a holiday in Eilat, on the Gulf of Aquaba, from which to tour both Israel and Egypt. By the time we completed the 'Holy Land' tour of Israel it was Christmas and quite cold and snowing in Jerusalem. We had visited the dignified

Berthold Fyvel Street in Tel-Aviv, named after Mick's father, and looked at the many graves on the Mount of Olives where he is buried. The Garden of Gethsemane with some old and gnarled olive trees is nearby. We saw all the holy places and entered the Mosque of Omar. My niece Louisa was staying in a Kibbutz near Jerusalem, she had very much enjoyed the agricultural work, the early rising and the camaraderie. During our stay in Israel we saw no evidence of trouble. Mick's view of the present situation is conveyed by slightly misquoting the Judgement of Solomon "and the King said 'let the living land be divided' ". Mick recalls that in 1936, Lord Peel and his fellow commissioners, who included Sir Harold Morris, son of Sir Malcolm Morris, St. Mary's first dermatologist, recommended Palestine be divided between Zionists and Arabs. The British Government would not have it.

We returned to Eilat and stayed at the Sonesta Hotel in Taba, then a disputed territory between Israel and Egypt and now handed over to Egypt. Here the weather was quite warm and sunny; we bathed in the pool and even in the sea. Then Mick and I crossed the frontier into Egypt. A very, very old Mercedes car and likewise an elderly Bedouin driver were waiting to take us to a tiny airport inside Sinai from which a small plane would fly us to Cairo. When the road inclined upwards, the driver would not change gear, but allowed the engine to chug on in top, the car ascending more and more slowly. However, the driver's acumen never failed, the summit of the road was always reached just before the engine might have stalled. As we proceeded into the desert it became colder and colder and I began to shiver, whereupon the Bedouin covered me with his coat seemingly as old as the car and probably, as I thought, home to creepy-crawlies, but I was grateful to have it over me. The scenery became wilder and more grandiose. I had visions of a sudden swoop by bandits, of abduction or worse — instead we were safely deposited at the airport. Our Cairo hotel was on the banks of the Nile and from the balcony of the high-up room, in the distance, Mick could see the pyramids. In the Cairo Museum were the Tutankhamun treasures, missed in London. Later we saw Tutankhamun's tomb in the Valley of the Kings when sailing from Aswan to Luxor on a Nile boat called Tot. We were pleased to have combined in one long visit the historical and venerable sights and stories of Israel and Ancient Egypt.

The very last meeting we attended was two years ago at St. Moritz organised by the American Dermatological Association. The president was Dr Jolly who had looked after us in New Orleans. The venue was the Palace Hotel. Many years ago, the writer Willie

Frischauer, then a patient, presented me with his book entitled '*A Hotel is Like a Woman*' in which he described a dozen of the world's most famous hotels and their glittering clientele. The Palace Hotel in St. Moritz was one of them. As St. Moritz is fairly high up in the Swiss Engadine, we arranged to arrive two days before the meeting to allow for acclimatisation. On checking in the hotel the receptionist beamed "You are the first guests of our summer season". When signing the register, Mick was in mind to put 'Duke and Duchess of Bournemouth' or something similar. The first evening, there being hardly any guests, the Palace's celebrated *maître d'hôtel* along with a bevy of waiters, hovered over our table, treating us as if we were really royal!

After St. Moritz we went on to Davos; although it was in the middle of July, a sudden snowstorm carpeted everything in white. On an excursion to Liechtenstein the coach passed through Klosters where the young Royals like to ski and we learnt that it was Sir Arthur Conan Doyle who had introduced skiing into Switzerland. The castle in Liechtenstein, perched on the mountainside, looked like a film set for 'Count Dracula' (though Bram Stoker was apparently inspired by an ancient Scottish castle). In Davos, for one special day, rides on the cable-cars became free — a good opportunity to ascend to the mountain-tops even though I could not fully appreciate the views owing to my visual defect. In the past Davos had been a centre for sanatoria looking after the tuberculous. Happily, that need has now gone.

Chapter 23

The Albany, Manor Road, Bournemouth

Miss M. K. Ashby, one-time principal of Hillcroft College, whom I have previously mentioned, settled down in Bledington with her friend Miss Margaret Phillips who had been principal of Borthwick Training College for Teachers which she initiated soon after the war and who was awarded the OBE for her services. The two ladies on their retirement bought the Home Farm in this Cotswold village along with two barns, many outhouses and a small orchard, all in a dilapidated condition. They set about renovating and refurbishing the buildings one by one. This was an uphill struggle as materials, licences and builders were then very difficult to come by. I remember Miss Ashby showing me with pride an old stone fireplace whose carvings and mouldings were uncovered in the course of the work.

Bledington is less known than other Cotswold villages, maybe because it is off the beaten track. However, it has similar mellow-golden stone buildings, with gables, mullioned windows and stone-tiled roofs. It also possesses a fine old church. Bledington is reached by turning right, off the London—Cheltenham road at Burford, driving down the lovely High Road, crossing the Windrush by an ancient bridge and then proceeding towards Stow-on-the-Wold. Before Stow is reached a minor road on the right through the small village of Idbury leads to Bledington. In *"The Changing English Village, 1066—1914"* Miss Ashby has traced its history. She was also awarded the James Tait Black prize for a biography of her father, active in the life of Cotswold villages at the turn of the century.

Mick and I often visited Bledington and were always pleased to enter, however briefly, into the life of an English village. We even considered purchasing one of the converted barns as a second home, but, on reflection, did not pursue the idea at that time, because we could ill afford such a venture. However, much later, in the early 1970s our thoughts again turned towards a second home. The Harley Street flat, which was really quite small, was bursting at the seams. Every time I opened a cupboard some of the contents spilled over me. It had become necessary to off-load some of our belongings. We began looking in the New Forest villages like Minstead, familiar from wartime days, but, finding nothing suitable, moved on to Bournemouth. Here we settled for a flat in the Albany, a tower-block on the East Cliff overlooking the sea and secured it before price rises had really taken off.

With her husband in Bournemouth

Today is Sunday, May 27th 1990. For nearly the whole month we have had uninterrupted sunshine. The beach is crowded as on a sunny August day and quite a number of people are sunbathing. Whoops of delight from the bucket and spade brigade echo in our ears as they dash (like lemmings) down the zigzag path of the cliff to the beach. What could be more attractive to the children than fine golden sands on a lovely day!